CHAN

Dr Radhakrishnan Pillai is the bestselling author of *Inside Chanakya's Mind* and *Chatur Chanakya and the Himalayan Problem*. He has researched Kautilya's *Arthashastra* extensively and has a master's degree in Sanskrit. He is the deputy director of the Chanakya International Institute of Leadership Studies (CIILS), University of Mumbai.

RADHAKRISHNAN PILLAI

CHANAKYA
AND THE
ART
OF
WAR

PORTFOLIO
PENGUIN

An imprint of Penguin Random House

PORTFOLIO

USA | Canada | UK | Ireland | Australia
New Zealand | India | South Africa | China

Portfolio is part of the Penguin Random House group of companies
whose addresses can be found at global.penguinrandomhouse.com

Published by Penguin Random House India Pvt. Ltd
7th Floor, Infinity Tower C, DLF Cyber City,
Gurgaon 122 002, Haryana, India

Penguin
Random House
India

First published in Portfolio by Penguin Random House India 2019

ISBN 9780143442899

Typeset in Adobe Caslon Pro by Manipal Digital Systems, Manipal
Printed at Thomson Press India Ltd, New Delhi

www.penguin.co.in

MIX
Paper
FSC   FSC® C010615

*To Chanakya—the foremost expert on the art of war.
Even today, the* Arthashastra *continues to guide military
leadership on war and strategic thinking.*

*Also, to all the experts and war gurus across generations
who knew that the ultimate aim of war is peace.*

Contents

Contents

Prologue

We are constantly at war.

It may be an external war—at our workplaces, our homes, amongst friends, relatives and/or with the government and its systems.

It may be an internal war—inside our heads, with time, with decisions, with what is right and what is wrong.

This is unavoidable when we live in a world full of different people and different views. From the day we are born to the day we die, the external or internal wars will continue. From womb to tomb, we will always face difficult choices.

After a point, everyone realizes that they cannot walk away from such wars. Everyone has to fight—some win, some lose. This is where the difference in our attitude towards the war becomes known. We either accept defeat, or fight on to emerge a winner.

Most of us often compromise and give up. It is a good feeling, although temporary, that there was no bloodshed, that we avoided facing an extreme situation. But later, when we sit down and analyse, we realize that we have actually lost the war in the name of compromise.

The problem continues to exist. Sooner than later, it re-emerges in a different way. The quick-fix of compromise is temporary in nature because we have not fixed the leak. The tooth now requires an extraction. That one rotten apple has already spoilt the whole bunch.

We must make sure we win the war once and for all, rather than be under the illusion that a compromise has closed the issue.

The art of winning a war *can* be learnt by understanding some rules and then applying them in a practical manner to real-life situations. There are various formulae and techniques. Just because we have never been exposed to a war does not mean the 'art of war' is not meant for us.

Swami Tejomayanandaji, the spiritual giant from Chinmaya Mission, says: 'If you don't stand up for something, you will fall for everything.'*

True that.

---

* Lecture on the Bhagavadgita, Chennai, 2016

Are we all just living a life of compromise and adjustment? Have we become so weak that we cannot even voice our views? Have we forgotten the skills of negotiations and strategy?

Let us not simply allow life to happen to us, let us make life happen according to our wishes. We can decide what we want, and yes, we can emerge a winner. The good news is that there is a method and a system to do this.

It starts with building some basic leadership qualities. Yes, the answer lies here.

Leaders are strong men and women who stood up with conviction, squared their shoulders and faced the challenges that came their way. They were the only hope when others around them felt hopeless. They had nothing else but tremendous will power. World history is never complete without the stories of such great leaders from various nations and backgrounds. Initially, they were ordinary people, but their extraordinary leadership qualities made them shine in situations that were challenging and difficult.

Today, the life stories of such leaders guide us. They inspire us. They bring hope and possibilities. They are the guiding beacons of societies. Their stories must be told to our children. They should be discussed at dinner tables, their books should be read by all, and more research should be done on these great men and women.

Emerging as a winner in war is not just the work of the military and armed forces. It can be part of our basic nature. If every individual is taught the art of war, she/he will be better equipped to focus on the means and the ends towards which they are working so hard. Winning a war requires many skills. Studying our opponent, understanding human psychology, the right timing and place, keeping motivation levels up—all these and more.

If we master the art of war, we can be successful in every field of life. As sportspersons, we will win medals; as corporate executives, we will achieve our targets; as government officials, we will execute all projects successfully, and as parents, we will bring up a healthy generation of children who have tremendous self-confidence and lead successful careers and lives.

In Nathalia Crane's words:

You cannot choose your battlefield,
God does that for you;
But you can plant a standard
Where a standard never flew

This is so true. Most of us are not prepared when a problem emerges. We are not ready at all. It hits us like a storm and can destroy us if we aren't prepared.

So friends, let us now look at the story of one such great man who inspired generations. A person who emerged as a leader at every stage of life. A leadership guru. A strategist. A nationalist. A guru, a teacher, a scholar and an author.

Yes, we are talking about Chanakya.

The person who reshaped Bharat, when the nation faced one of its most challenging times—a broken internal state and a powerful invader hell-bent on capturing our lands.

In such a dire situation, Chanakya did not give up. He mastered strategy and tactics. He specialized in the art of war, and even wrote a book for future generations to refer to—*Kautilya's Arthashastra*.

In this book, *Chanakya and the Art of War*, we will be taking you on a journey. The journey of Chanakya's life experiences and challenges. We go back to his era and time. We draw inspiration and learn from his wisdom.

This exploration is also about India as a nation. Although Chanakya, just as everyone else does, had limited time on earth, his ideas did not die with him. For generations, kings and rulers across the globe have applied Chanakya's theories and rules. And so we will learn about such people who have kept 'Chanakya Niti' alive in our society.

This book is your friend in this journey. As a reader, I would like you to assess your life challenges and apply the techniques and tactics given here. After all, no journey is complete till it becomes a part of who you are.

Introduction

Chanakya was a teacher of war strategies.

He wrote down everything he had studied about war and war techniques in the *Arthashastra*, which contains 6000 sutras (formulae) on how to win over the enemy. Among the fifteen books contained in the *Arthashastra*, seven relate to warfare and battle craft. Additionally, there are many other ideas that he propounded in his other book, *Chanakya Niti*.

In the present book, we will decode Chanakya's war secrets, as relevant to our personal and professional lives. Be it the army that is fighting soldiers across the border, the police dealing with internal challenges in the nation, the politician planning to win elections, or the common man fighting for survival, Chanakya understands it all.

This book covers many stories from Chanakya's life—how he defeated Alexander the Great, how he figured out the internal problem of defeating the arrogant Dhana Nanda, one of the most powerful kings of the Magadh Empire, and many more anecdotes. These display his foresight and active implementation of plans.

The book also covers some philosophical aspects of war, such as the war that goes on inside us every moment, among the different types of wars we encounter in life. It explains one of the most famous war theories of Chanakya—*Sama, Dana, Danda* and *Bheda*.

We will look at the game of chess, the ultimate war board game still played today. We will also study about the various ancient gurus of war whom Chanakya had referred to and whom he learnt from.

We will learn about Vijigishu as well, the Indian who was a possible world conqueror, who has been mentioned in the *Arthashastra*.

Chanakya's wisdom about the different types of powers one should know about in order to become a winner are explained in this book, because war is all about power, and who understood power better than Chanakya?

At the end, there are certain tips that you can practise to win the daily battles of life.

Make sure you read this book, page to page, and word to word. Chanakya will guide you as your mentor and coach.

Welcome to the battlefield.

1

How Chanakya
Defeated Alexander

One resolute in his undertakings does not stop
without completing his work.

—*Arthashastra* (7.8.13)

In war, it does not matter who your opponent is, whether
you are stronger or weaker than the enemy, or if you
have better weapons or a larger army. What matters is
your determination.

Mighty empires can collapse by the will of a single
man. The most powerful tool against your opponent is
your faith in yourself. Such a person will stop at nothing
till he achieves his goal.

This is the story of two determined men. These were
the men who changed the course of world history.

One was a warrior—a young, determined leader out to conquer the world. He was nothing short of being an incarnation of the divine. Many considered him to be a god on earth. He was swift and fast. He had a powerful army along with nerves of steel. His name alone could rouse fear in the minds of the enemy. This is the story of Alexander the Great.

The other one was a teacher—a person who had perfected the art of politics. He had with him the wisdom of the ages. He was a revered scholar, a revolutionary philosopher and thinker, and a formidable strategist. He was a sharp and intelligent man. His name commanded respect. If he decided to do something, nothing could stop him. This is the story of Chanakya, the Legend.

These two men lived in two different parts of the world during the same era. They came from two successful civilizations. One was from the cradle of Western philosophy—Greece. The other was nurtured in the land of knowledge—Bharat.

World history is not complete without the story of these two resolute men. Their lives are an inspiration for generations. The war against Alexander in Bharat was not just a military war; it was philosophical, it was about an idea and a way of life, which could be followed by others. These ideas do not die with time; they become perfect when they are tested over time.

Alexander was born in Macedonia, Greece, in 356 BC, to King Philip II and Queen Olympias.[*] Alexander showed impressive courage and promise from a young age. To tutor Alexander, his father called on Aristotle, who trained him in literature, science, medicine and philosophy. Alexander followed his father's dream to conquer the lands beyond their kingdom. His armies defeated formidable foes and marched on under his leadership through Persia to make him king of the land. There was a belief about Alexander that he was a divine being who had come to rule the world.

His goal was to conquer Asia, which was a challenge. Thus far, he had not lost a single war. That was a mighty feat in itself. An undefeated army meant a confident ruthless army. Soon, he was at the borders of Bharatvarsha. He expected a heroic entry in the land. However, the terrain and region were completely new to him and his army. He was not aware of the prevalent circumstances and conditions of this new place. King Ambhi, ruler of the kingdom where modern Pakistan is situated, was the first king in the subcontinent who faced Alexander. Overwhelmed by Alexander's force, Ambhi surrendered immediately.

---

[*] https://www.history.com/topics/ancient-history/alexander-the-great

This was good enough for Alexander. The next king on his path was Porus, or Parwateshwar, who then ruled the region of modern Punjab.

Porus was a man of tremendous self-respect. He did not want to surrender easily or to accept the rule of Alexander. He gave his best in the battle against Alexander. Unfortunately, Porus was defeated. Alexander took stock of the battle as a lesson learnt. At times, when we meet a good competitor, we start respecting the enemy. Alexander had met one such king. The dignity and the moral superiority shown by Porus made Alexander respect him.

The vanquished Porus was captured and brought before Alexander by his soldiers on his orders. When Porus arrived, he stood tall and showed a kind of grace that Alexander had never seen before. Instead of ordering to kill or put him behind bars, Alexander asked Porus a question.

'Now that you are a defeated king, how should I treat you?'

Alexander expected Porus to ask for pardon or to be released from Alexander's camp.

Porus's reply shocked him.

'You should treat me as a king treats another king,' he said.

Rather than showing fear of being executed or killed, Porus was demanding and commanding respect. For

Alexander, this was a completely new experience. He was not aware of Bharatvarsha's version of dharma yudh, an ethical practice of war. When a king is defeated, he is not killed. That happens only in extreme conditions. One lets go of the defeated enemy. A king should respect another king. Morality demands that.

So instead of becoming angry with Porus, Alexander befriended him. He was introduced to one of the new rules of war based on Indian ethics—never hate your enemy; rather, respect him.

This was only the beginning of Alexander's journey in the region. He was yet to face one of the greatest challenges that he would come across. This time, it did not come from a king. It was a teacher who would prevent him from making any further inroads into the region.

Bharatvarsha as a nation was self-sufficient. Geographically, its location and climatic conditions are very favourable to its populace. It has regular seasons like summer and winter, and receives plenty of rainfall. The flora and fauna of the country at the time had numerous varieties of fruits and vegetables to offer. There was enough for everyone for basic survival. Teachers and spiritual gurus in the land always taught the citizens to be detached from the world and to seek moksha and self-enlightenment. Our ideologies spread across our neighbouring lands through trade routes and other business opportunities. As is human nature, there were some who were greedy for more power and wealth.

Bharatvarsha was, at the time, divided into sixteen regional kingdoms. All of them were busy fighting one other. For centuries, there had been unending battles in the country.

Chanakya, then a teacher at Takshashila University, was aware of Alexander. In his wisdom, he had concluded that Alexander's conquest of the land was a threat to our culture. We had always believed in the concept of 'atithi devo bhava' and had always welcomed visitors as gods. However, invaders were different. They did not come as visitors. They came to loot and destroy.

Chanakya's deep insights into human psychology made him realize that if Alexander were to conquer the region, its impact would be more than just having a new ruler for the land. He recognized the threat posed to the ancient knowledge and wisdom that Bharatvarsha had always preserved and held so close to its heart. The master strategist in him started putting together a scheme to thwart Alexander's plans. It is important to note here that Chanakya was no king; he did not have an army.

He decided to approach the most powerful of kingdoms in the country with his plans. He wanted all the kings to unite as one force and fight against Alexander. A united front against any external threat is a formidable opponent indeed.

With that approach in mind, he appealed to Dhana Nanda, the most powerful king of those days, the ruler of Magadh, who also had the largest army.

Dhana Nanda was in no mood to listen to Chanakya. Instead of supporting him, he dismissed his worries. His priorities were limited to Magadh and he was confident that when Alexander reached Magadh, he would defeat the invader.

Chanakya tried to persuade him by explaining the larger picture to the mighty king.

'If our head is hit, our hands come to its rescue and protect it. When there is dust in the eyes, the fingers will rub it out of the eyes.'

He tried to raise the issue of equality amongst the citizens of the land of Bharat, pointing out that Magadh was a part of Bharat.

Dhana Nanda paid no heed to the master strategist. Instead, he insulted him and pushed him out of the court. This angered Chanakya a lot. Deeming it an unsuitable time to set Dhana Nanda right, he moved on to the main problem—Alexander.

What was the alternative route?

There were many smaller kings and kingdoms at the time. So he started approaching these kings and told them about the problem staring them in the face.

Just like Dhana Nanda, some other kings too did not support the master teacher. Some just heard him out without doing anything about it. Some others, though, extended their support. Just as individual drops of water make up an ocean, slowly and steadily, one by one, those supporting Chanakya's plan started to grow in number and strength. Elephants were unique to the army. While Alexander's army had good horses, they did not know how to tackle the stupendous might of war elephants. Thus, the combined strength of all the kings in the region became a larger, more powerful force to reckon with.

Having made Ambhi his ally and defeating as powerful a king as Porus, Alexander was confident of winning over the rest of the country. He had no inkling of Chanakya's plans.

Chanakya had a number of students under his tutelage, both male and female. They were trained in various subjects required to run and defend a kingdom. Chandragupta Maurya was one of them. Chanakya also understood the use of a good espionage system as a source of information and better strategy planning.

Chanakya's spies were trained in human psychology. When Chanakya realized that he wanted to gather information regarding the enemy, he sent forth his male spies. They entered the enemy camp and tried to understand their modus operandi. They were wonderstruck with Alexander. They came back and reported their impressions to their leader, who simply dismissed their reports about the weapons, the strength of the soldiers and Alexander's persona. Chanakya was not impressed with the information that they had brought. He explained to them that this information wasn't new. When different spies brought back nothing new, he decided to try out the female spies, also known as the Vishkanyas.

The women came back with a strange insight about Alexander's army. They reported that the army was homesick. When Chanakya asked them to explain how they had reached this conclusion, the Vishkanyas reported that when they entered the enemy camp under various pretences, the girls were never looked at with lust, as is usually expected. The soldiers had looked at them with a look a father might have for his children. The girls reminded them of their families left behind at home. The spies suggested that this was crucial information.

Chanakya understood that these soldiers who had been away from their homes, fighting, for so many years were missing their families. The master strategist then started playing with the minds of the soldiers. He sent out more Vishkanyas and made the enemy soldiers feel nostalgic remembering their own homes far away. Right enough, a distinct decrease in the zeal of the soldiers became noticeable.

When the time came, Alexander forced his army to march ahead. His army was shocked to see the huge army and war elephants facing them. Alexander's soldiers were hesitant to fight. They wanted to go back to Greece. Alexander was surprised by their reactions. They turned back after a point.

Thus, one of the greatest warriors of all times, who had been ready to conquer the world, was thwarted by a different kind of warfare.

This is what Chanakya's art of war is all about.

You may not have any power. However, if you have a powerful will, coupled with strategy, you can defeat anyone. That is what the power of thinking is all about— the most powerful weapon in the world.

As the saying in the Indian army goes: Battles are not fought on the battlefield, but in the minds of the generals.

Chanakya played on the minds of Alexander and his troops to win the war.

2

How Chanakya Defeated Dhana Nanda, the Most Powerful King of the Magadh Empire

The king, conversant with the science of politics, acquiring land from other kings, secures a special advantage over confederates and enemies.

—*Arthashastra* (7.10.38)

The era was fourth century BC. Situated in the modern state of Bihar, Magadh, one of the most powerful kingdoms of the era, was ruled by some of the best kings from the Nanda dynasty.

It was a huge kingdom with a large army and a legacy of nine generations of kings belonging to the Nanda dynasty. It takes generations of powerful rulers to make such a kingdom. A mix of a good ruler and efficient advisors and ministers of the king's court is essential to build an empire. Various socio-economic factors also contribute to the shaping of a great civilization. A disciplined military force, a defendable and daunting fortress, happy citizens and friendly neighbours equally contribute to the prosperity of a kingdom.

Magadh, with Pataliputra as its capital, possessed all the requisite essentials that made it one of the best governed kingdoms during those days.

However, family leadership and dynasty rule has its own advantages and disadvantages. If the succeeding leader is good, everything will continue to be progressive. But if the next leader is not capable, or does not have the right attitude, the empire can begin to collapse. Everything boils down to the right kind of leader, guided by the most able ministers.

Magadh had the good fortune to have everything right for eight generations of kings of the Nanda dynasty. Enter the ninth king, Dhana Nanda, and things began to shake a bit. Born with a silver spoon, Dhana Nanda was deemed to be a capable leader of his people.

Unfortunately, not all able leaders turn out to be good. Some talented leaders have fallen due to arrogance. As was the case with Dhana Nanda. He was smart and charming, he had family legacy on his side, and when the time came, it anointed him with the royal crown being placed on his head.

Usually, when the new ruler is from the ruling family, there are a lot of expectations from other concerned parties. Everyone expected Dhana Nanda to become the next 'ideal leader'. Destiny, however, had something else in store for the kingdom of Magadh.

Dhana Nanda enjoyed his newfound kingly power and grew so blinded by it that he soon started to neglect his responsibilities. As they say, power corrupts, and absolute power corrupts absolutely. Instead of looking after the welfare of his subjects, he spent more time in pleasurable activities. Indulging in entertainment and enjoying his time with women, drinking, turning a blind eye to the problems which a king is required to solve—all this became a daily routine. Indiscipline became a way of life for the king.

The kingdom was powerful, but the king was misusing his power. Soon, the leader and leadership were being questioned by one and all. The public had begun noticing this weakness in their ruler.

Magadh had, fortunately, a good set of ministers with able heads managing different parts of its welfare and economy. Even while the head of the kingdom was losing himself in the pleasures of being a king, his ministers were serving the kingdom and its citizens with much fervour. Magadh also boasted of great teachers and thinkers from every field. This was one of the greatest assets of the kingdom. Their knowledge capital was powerful because of the presence of capable ministers, one among them being Chanak. An able minister and a teacher of political science, he was a highly respected guru. A strong-headed person, he had high hopes of Dhana Nanda. He expected him to be made of the same mould as his ancestors, having high moral standards.

From time to time, Chanak went to the king and gave him some sound advice about how a leader should behave, about what the roles and responsibilities of a leader are. He used to frequently quote from the scriptures, which defined a leader as one having high moral superiority and integrity.

Unfortunately, Dhana Nanda turned a deaf ear to all advice. The king believed that he was all-powerful. He would listen to elders and teachers as decorum demanded, but would reserve his choice in following their advice.

Chanak was distressed about the king's growing indifference. According to him, the kingdom was facing economic problems purely due to the irresponsible behaviour of the king. Therefore, if the kingdom had to improve and maintain its glory, it had to start with Dhana Nanda himself.

Dhana Nanda used to laugh at everything that was said to him by way of advice. He was not serious about the status of the kingdom.

One day, things took a drastic turn.

Chanak walked into the court of Dhana Nanda and announced that he would be forced to awaken the public against the king if the king did not mend his ways. His subjects were becoming restless and their king's indifference was only fuelling the spark.

The king became furious. He removed Chanak from the role of the royal advisor.

Chanak did not really care for the royal position he held. He cared more for the people and their happiness. This became a personal war now. A war between the king and a teacher.

The little boy Chanakya, son of Chanak, was not aware of what his father was doing.

After being insulted by Dhana Nanda, Chanak went to the marketplace and made a public speech. He wanted everyone to stand up for their rights as citizens. He wanted the king to diligently do his duties. He brought out the negligence and corrupt practices of the king in the open.

When the news reached the king, concerns were raised in the corridors of power. Many ministers had been supporting Dhana Nanda in his wrong practices. Their personal interests were under threat with this new development. They suggested that the problem should be nipped in the bud. Overnight, a plan was made to silence the movement being led by Chanak.

A civil war was on its way.

That night, something strange happened. While Chanak was preparing to address a few more public meetings to spread awareness among the citizens of Magadh, a group of soldiers came and took hold of him. Dhana Nanda had given strict orders to eliminate him. In the dead of the night, Chanak was hanged from a tree in the middle of the marketplace. The next day, when the people came to the marketplace, they saw the dead body and were terrified.

Dhana Nanda was happy with his soldiers for executing the plan. His plan had sent out a strong message to the public. No one would dare stand against the king any more. As he had intended, the people did not know how to respond. If a great teacher such as Chanak could be killed so openly, what chance did a common man have? The people of Magadh were paralysed with fear.

This act of killing a teacher by a member of the Nanda family was least expected. The Nanda dynasty was the first to respect and appreciate the best teachers on their side. But here was a king who had killed a teacher for showing him the right path.

There were many good teachers in Pataliputra, who were aware of the good intentions of Chanak. Hearing about his unfortunate and untimely execution, they were sure his family would be at high risk.

As soon as the news reached the teacher community, the teachers rushed to Chanak's wife. They were concerned about her safety. Chanak's wife was a strong lady and did not want to abandon her husband's cause. She did agree to send away their son, Chanakya, to protect him. The teachers decided that Chanakya would be sent to Takshashila University, which was far away from his hometown. There were teachers in Takshashila who were Chanak's friends. They would ensure his stay and education at the university.

When young Chanakya was told about the turn of events, he asked them for the reasons behind this. Learning about his father's fate, he became furious. But what could a little boy do? There was nothing more than anger that he could express. After a little persuasion from the other teachers and his own mother, Chanakya agreed to leave Pataliputra for a better and safer future.

On reaching Takshashila, he was immediately admitted to the university. The teachers there had already heard about the greatness of his father, and how he stood strong against the mighty king. However, Chanakya had not come to Takshashila to simply stand in the shadow of his father's glory.

The next few years in the life of Chanakya were both the worst and the best days of his life. He missed his family. He was plagued with concern for his mother whom he had left alone right after his father's demise. He often thought about her welfare. For years, he did not hear any news about her.

Takshashila helped him divert his attention from the past to the present. He had access to the knowledge and wisdom of the greatest living teachers. Each teacher in Takshashila was a living legend. They were the best in their respective subjects. Bharatvarsha in those days was known for its wealth of wisdom. The teachers in universities such as Takshashila and Nalanda were advisors to the best kings from different parts of the world.

Among the thousands of subjects that were taught in the university, Chanakya chose his favourite— political science. It was called 'raja niti' and 'raja vidya', meaning 'knowledge for the kings'. The technical name for political science according to ancient Indian culture was 'arthashastra'.

There were many teachers who taught arthashastra. There were many books written on the subject. Chanakya spent most of his time studying and understanding the various theories of arthashastra as given by these teachers, called purvacharyas. He was engrossed in the techniques of political science as he explored the different teachings of purvacharyas. He also liked the war techniques used by them. He read and reread many books on warfare, strategy, military science and policies which gave him an insight into dealing with friends and enemies of the nation. He made it his goal to master the subject of political science.

Time flew by, and he even received the best student award. The university was also proud to have such an excellent student as him. A teacher mentioned that this boy would make his father proud. They seemed to have the same interest in bringing glory to any kingdom they supported.

Chanakya, even as a student, had his own, independent views on every subject that was discussed. He was a logician, a strategist, a critical thinker and an analyst all rolled into one. On completing his education, he was asked to continue in Takshashila as a professor. He was one of the youngest teachers at the university, but students eagerly waited for his lectures. It was a normal sight to see other teachers also attending his classes. They tried to learn from him. His style was unique. His in-depth analysis was worthy of setting forth the best intellect to seek deeper wisdom. He encouraged questions from his students.

He often used to tell his students to question every answer. He urged them not to take any answer at face value. He encouraged them to learn to think critically and logically. As long as they questioned whatever they were taught till they were satisfied with the answer, he had done a good job. He told them that he intended to create leaders, not followers. And the best way to do that was to be an original thinker.

University debates were incomplete without discussing ideas that Chanakya taught in his class. Even though he was teaching a group of students who were learning political science, the students in the other classes knew about his lessons. That was the power of his teaching and ideas.

All good things come to an end, though. One day, a messenger came with a letter from Pataliputra. It was addressed to this young teacher who had won the hearts of everyone over the years: 'Your time has come. Now return to Pataliputra. You need to fulfil a bigger duty. The Magadh kingdom awaits you. All that you have learnt and taught at Takshashila need practical application in Magadh. Your theories need to meet practice. Your war ideas need to be implemented here. Come back as soon as you get this letter.'

This letter was sent by a senior teacher from Magadh, a dear friend of his father Chanak. He was one of the teachers who had helped young Chanakya flee from Pataliputra.

Tears came to the eyes of the young man. He clearly recollected the day when, as a helpless child, he had left everything he loved. This included his dear mother. Anger and frustration about those events blazed in his heart when he thought of Dhana Nanda. And now the time had come for Chanakya to go back and fulfil his life's mission. He was ready and the road towards Pataliputra never looked so welcoming.

As soon as he reached the city gates, he found himself going down memory lane. He visited the school where he had studied, the place where he used to play, the houses of his friends, the village temple and the marketplace. He observed all these with new eyes. But something did not seem right everywhere he went. In the eyes of everyone he saw, there was sadness and pain. As if it had been hit by a natural calamity, the city wore a deserted look. There seemed to be a sense of grief deep within everyone. What had happened to Pataliputra, the renowned capital of the great Magadh kingdom? This was not what he had seen when he had left.

Chanakya had no time to analyse the situation. His legs took him speedily in the direction of his house. He wanted to go and meet his mother. That was his only aim when he reached his hometown. He started to run as soon as he reached the lane of his house. But what he saw there was shocking. The house was in a dilapidated condition. It seemed completely broken down. No one appeared to be staying there. Chanakya rushed into the inner rooms, hoping to see his mother. After searching every room, he realized she was not around. Like a lost child searching for his mother, he started crying and yelling. It took him some time to compose himself and gather his senses. By this time, some neighbours had arrived.

Chanakya was known as Vishnugupta. This was his original name. An aunt who lived in his neighbourhood, now old, rushed towards him. He asked her about his mother. Everyone was silent. When he repeatedly asked for his mother, they finally broke the silence and informed him that she was no more. As if thunder from the skies had struck him on the head, Chanakya lost his bearing.

When he came to, he asked the aunt to tell him what had happened. His mother had lost her will to live after Chanakya's departure. Her husband and her son were her strength. She lost her mental strength in the days after Chanakya's departure. When the end was near, she left a message for her son, saying that Chanakya would come back one day and be the salvation for Magadh. He would restore its glory and his mother's blessings would always be with him. Chanakya did not know how to stop his tears. He was an orphan now.

A familiar-looking person walked into the house. Chanakya looked up to see who it was. A face so radiant and brilliant that everyone would at once stand up with respect and reverence. It was the same teacher and friend of his father who had sent Chanakya to Takshashila. The one who had written the letter to Chanakya and called him back from Takshashila. He reminded him about the purpose of his return.

'Chanakya, you are now Acharya Chanakya from Takshashila, a gurukul the world looks up to. I had sent you there to study from the best and become the best. I am glad that you have exceeded our expectations. You have made Magadh and your parents proud. Now you have a bigger role to fulfil. Your father and mother are gone, but you have to serve your other mother—the motherland. Our Bharat Mata requires your knowledge in the field of raja niti. All that you have mastered in the field of political science needs to be practised here. You will have to dethrone Dhana Nanda and establish a new order of kings. You have to recreate the golden era of our Bharatvarsha. You have to teach raja vidya to the new generation of leaders. You have to write your own arthashastra. And till that happens, you will not rest.'

After a few days of grief and acceptance of his situation, Chanakya began to plan his strategy to defeat Dhana Nanda. He was aware that it was not going to be easy. He was not a king and he did not have an army of his own. The only advantage he had over Dhana Nanda was his knowledge and his ability as a strategic thinker.

The teacher who had brought back Chanakya to Pataliputra knew he was ready to take on Dhana Nanda, but he also understood that young Chanakya required mentoring and guidance. He reminded the distraught disciple of some simple rules of war and strategy.

- *Never hate your enemy. Your strategy should not be guided by hatred. Hatred towards the enemy can cloud your judgement. In war, the greatest weapon is a calm and composed mind.*
- *Frustration will only lead to self-destruction. Do not let go of the enemy, as that would be a cowardly act, but hitting back in frustration will not bring any results for your endeavour.*
- *Plan your strategy in silence. Keep the enemy confused and wondering about what you are doing.*
- *In war, there is something called right timing. Just wait for the right time to execute your plan.*
- *Study the present situation and conditions of the environment.*
- *Defeating your enemy should be your primary goal, not killing them. They are not the same thing. Killing the leader will make another person from his team take up the leadership position. Then you will have to kill him too. Then another person will be ready to fight with you. The story will continue.*

When Chanakya asked for advice as to his next step, the teacher suggested that he continue to be a teacher but at a well-known gurukul in Pataliputra, where children of ministers of the court and the royal family went to study. That way, he would be able to get information about all that happened in Magadh.

It took a few years for Chanakya to devise a perfect plan for his war against Dhana Nanda. But his mind was continuously working. When the right time came, he had a deeper understanding about the power politics at play in the kingdom.

Chanakya concluded that defeating Dhana Nanda required a three-point strategy.

1. He needed a new king to replace Dhana Nanda. One may defeat an existing king, but the question then arises as to who will be the next king? If the new leader is not ready, it can lead to a stage of 'no leadership'. And that could lead to worse situations. At times, a bad leader is better than no leader. So, he decided to create a new leader along the way. He identified Chandragupta as the next king of the Magadh kingdom, who would eventually become the first emperor of a united Bharatvarsha. Chandragupta was trained and mentored on leadership by Chanakya himself.

2. He needed to build an army of his own. He had studied a lot of theories on how to defeat the enemy in a war. He learnt that it was not possible to fight a war without an army. After he started teaching students in the gurukul of Magadh, he trained his students in warfare and created an army of his own, led by Chandragupta. He reduced his role to focus on being a strategist and coach to the newly formed young and energetic army.

3. He needed to assess the strength of the enemy. He knew that in the strength of the enemy lies his weakness. What was Dhana Nanda's strength? When he studied more about Dhana Nanda and his despicable practices, Chanakya realized that he still remained the king. He learnt that the biggest strength the bad king had was Amatya Rakshas, a capable and dedicated minister. Dhana Nanda also respected Amatya Rakshas and would never go against him. He trusted Amatya Rakshas like no one else. So, it was important to tackle him. Amatya Rakshas was so dedicated to Dhana Nanda that he would give up his life for him. He would not spare anyone who even thought of going against the king. This was the biggest challenge Chanakya faced. As a person, Amatya Rakshas was a great man. He was a scholar of

raja niti and an efficient administrator. He was a dream minister for any king. Chanakya respected Amatya Rakshas and knew that he was the best prime minister Magadh had ever had.

Chanakya thought deeply about how to defeat Dhana Nanda and, at the same time, make sure Amatya Rakshas was given his due respect. The latter was the main obstacle in the road to victory. Yet, no one could be more capable than him in administering the kingdom.

Then, an unforeseen event happened. A new problem arose.

Chanakya knew that even in the most challenging situation, if one is able to think clearly through it, one will find solutions to all problems.

He sat down to think calmly and an idea flashed through his mind. He figured out his strategy to defeat Dhana Nanda.

I will use one enemy against another.

The right time to attack Dhana Nanda had come. But the method to be used was going to be different. He got ready and went to meet Dhana Nanda himself. Face-to-face.

3

Chanakya's Way to Win over the Inner Enemy

An arrow, discharged by an archer, may kill or may not kill the person; but intellect operated by a wise man would kill even children in the womb.

—*Arthashastra* (10.6.51)

While living in Pataliputra, Chanakya was good friends with a classmate. Both enjoyed studying and discussing political science. They spent most of their time analysing various scenarios in political situations across the globe. Time passed by and they grew up. While the friend continued to stay and study in Pataliputra, Chanakya went to Takshashila. They reconnected after Chanakya came back.

The two friends enjoyed each other's company and even helped each other in their work. As luck would have it, the friend had secured a minister's post in Magadh. He was one of the young yet respected scholars of raja niti in Pataliputra. He was the blue-eyed boy of Amatya Rakshas.

Chanakya would often say that his friend would become the next prime minister of Magadh. That was the most desired and celebrated post any young boy could aspire to in power circles. But his friend always responded that Chanakya would be a better candidate for the post if he ever considered it.

Chanakya was clear about what he wanted to be. He told his friend that he would prefer being a kingmaker than a minister. He envisioned himself as the watchdog of the kingdom, if anything.

The time had come for Chanakya to meet Dhana Nanda face-to-face. It was now that he required his friend's help the most. He requested his friend to arrange for a meeting. His friend was alarmed and refused. He said that the king was very particular about whom he spent time with, and if he figured out that Chanakya was the son of Chanak, Chanakya could be in danger.

Once Chanakya assured him that the king wouldn't find out about his identity, his friend started thinking of ways to fix the meeting. When Chanakya questioned him, he clarified that he was not worried about his job; rather, for him, the nation came first. His friend admitted that Magadh was losing respect among the teaching community due to Dhana Nanda's behaviour. When Chanakya suggested that all teachers should protest against the king, his friend reminded him of what had happened to his own father. Sometimes the silence of the good is the reason for the success of the bad, was Chanakya's response.

His friend explained the situation at court to Chanakya. The ministers were trying their best to prioritize people's interests and keep the kingdom afloat. They had to watch over the king and his actions. It was difficult to understand the intentions of the ministers and teachers without being in the same position as they were.

Chanakya was curious about the secret method the ministers were using to run the kingdom under such a king, but his friend refused to divulge it. He provoked Chanakya to come into the fray and learn it for himself. Chanakya respected his friend for keeping the secrets of the court from a common teacher such as himself.

Chanakya admitted that his theories were no match for the problems of the real political world at times. His friend recognized Chanakya's humility and explained how the ministers were running the kingdom solely on the strength of one person, Amatya Rakshas, who guided all ministers, especially when the king put them under dharma sankat. He recollected some of the lessons of Amatya.

> There are choices in life. When you do not know what to do, think of the higher power called God. He has put us in a situation. We should not think too much. Just do our duty in the given situation.

His friend assured him that he would try to facilitate a meeting between Chanakya and the king. His friend warned Chanakya to keep his temper in check in front of the king. Chanakya knew that the real war is never fought outside. It is always fought within. The person who has self-control is the one who wins the war.

* * *

Ancient Indian tradition has many ideas about how to win over the 'inner enemy' before defeating the external one. Chanakya had taught his students the concept of 'indriya jaya', meaning control over the senses. The one who can control himself will finally win the war. Self-control is the foundation of the character of a winner in life.

Human beings have emotions and feelings. It is natural for a person to become emotional from time to time. However, when we allow our feelings to take over all our senses, it can become a major problem.

Have emotions. But do not become emotional.

Whenever feelings arise within you—watch them. Meditation is the method one can use to observe the thoughts and feelings inside us, to understand why and when they come and go. Only a meditative mind can achieve success in mastering one's emotions.

A mind which is calm and quiet can think clearly. One who develops such a state of mind is better equipped to formulate strategy. It is strategy that helps us defeat the enemy.

It does not matter if the enemy is big or small. What really matters is how you tackle your adversary. The quiet mind will automatically see through the problems facing it and know how to navigate through the challenges.

The quieter the mind, the better the strategy.

How does one develop the process of strategic thinking once you have a meditative mind? One needs to practise the science of thinking called 'aanvikshiki'.

Aanvikshiki is a special kind of knowledge meant for leaders. It means philosophy, according to various scholars. But Chanakya wanted his students to learn aanvikshiki to become good thinkers.

When our thinking is clear, we can achieve success in every field. Even in war, it is essential to have the objective clearly defined. Then, using the right strategy and tactics, one can win over the enemy.

What are the inner enemies of a person?

There are six of them, as given in the *Arthashastra*. These negative qualities corrupt our minds and distract us from achieving our goals. Chanakya would always explain these inner enemies to his students with a lot of examples. They are:

1. Kama (lust)—Lust for anything is not beneficial to anyone. There are many who have a lust for power. If that is what motivates a leader, he will not only destroy himself but also the whole kingdom.

2. Krodha (anger)—This is the greatest inner enemy. When we get carried away by anger, we are like a fire, which will burn everything around us. There are many good people who, in a fit

of anger, have destroyed things dear to them. Therefore, it is essential to manage our anger.

3. Lobha (greed)—This demands more attention than what we give it. Greed may exist not just for money, but also for power and position. Nature has provided us with everything we need. But when one becomes greedy, one starts demanding more than what is required and starts destroying nature to satiate one's greed.

4. Moha (attachment)—This is where the downfall of a leader begins. When it is time to give up power, many are not ready to do so easily. They become so attached to it that they feel they cannot live without it. In order to tackle attachment, we need to develop detachment. It is a detached leader who actually performs her/his duty well.

5. Mada (pride)—When pride enters our mind we lose humility. Arrogance sets in. And then begins our downfall. It boosts our ego and we start feeling superior to others around us. We close ourselves to other people's opinions and inputs. In the long run this leads to our destruction.

6. Matsarya (jealousy)—This is an emotion we often feel towards people who have achieved more than what we have. An inner fire keeps eroding our sense of contentment and leads to

frustration and loss of peace of mind, while the other person remains unaffected.

Chanakya used to make sure that his students were able to develop inner strength to win over these six inner enemies.

One never knows when these inner enemies take control of our minds. Only by being vigilant will one discover them inside us. Slowly, we need to remove each of them, one by one.

Once these inner enemies are removed, the mind becomes clear. There is no inner dirt left, and one can think better and bigger. The mind has the power to create anything it wants. But for that to happen, the basic foundation needed is a pure mind.

* * *

Dhana Nanda's biggest problem was that his mind had been corrupted by the six enemies inside him.

Chanakya knew that he was about to face one of the most powerful kings. His friend had managed to arrange a meeting for him. The reason Chanakya wanted to meet the king was to tell him of the external enemy about to enter the country—Alexander. He wanted to seek his help to form an alliance with other kingdoms and send the intruder back to Greece.

Chanakya realized that this wasn't the time to settle personal scores. The nation was at risk. He wanted to make Dhana Nanda aware of the bigger problem that faced them.

Dhana Nanda was known to dismiss meeting requests from scholars and teachers. When he was asked to meet Chanakya, one of the most intelligent teachers from the University of Takshashila, Dhana Nanda had no idea that he was the son of Chanak, the teacher he had killed many years ago. Howsoever reluctantly, he did agree to meet Chanakya briefly.

When Chanakya entered the king's court, Dhana Nanda asked him for the reason for the meeting. The moment Chanakya came face-to-face with the king, all the past memories came rushing back. But he did not allow the feeling of anger or hatred to show on his face. This was the kind of self-control Chanakya had to practise. He had to conquer the inner enemy before he could win over Dhana Nanda.

In a steady voice, Chanakya informed the king about the intruder who had come all the way from Greece to conquer our lands. He asked him for his support to defeat him. When Dhana Nanda realized that Alexander was far away from Magadh, he understood that the Greek invader would first have to win over the other kingdoms on his way before he could reach Magadh.

Dhana Nanda dismissed Chanakya's request by pointing out that Alexander would attack those other kingdoms anyway and Magadh need not be involved in that. They would fight when their own kingdom came under threat.

When Chanakya pointed out that Magadh's large and powerful army would face a stronger Greek army because they would have befriended or dethroned many kingdoms by the time they reached Magadh, Dhana Nanda's pride prevented him from understanding the seriousness of the issue. He ignored the impending threat and asked Chanakya not to waste the court's time with unfruitful discussions.

Chanakya was not ready to give up and urged the king to save the nation. He tried to remind him of his responsibility as one of the most powerful rulers of the nation. He pointed out that as one of the most respected leaders in all of Bharatvarsha, he needed to take up the challenge and form alliances with other kingdoms.

Dhana Nanda was furious with Chanakya because he was still addressing the king even after being asked to leave. His pride rendered him deaf to Chanakya's arguments and pleadings. He ordered the guards to take the teacher away, but Amatya Rakshas stepped up and asked the guards to let go of him as it was a rule of court to respect all teachers.

Dhana Nanda, overtaken by anger, insulted Chanakya and accused him of being too arrogant when he was only an ordinary teacher. This was the last straw and Chanakya decided to speak up for himself. He reminded Dhana Nanda that teachers are not ordinary people as they have the ability to create and destroy leaders. He reprimanded the king for failing to perform his duty towards his people in the light of an impending threat and for his arrogance. As a mark of defiance, Chanakya opened his shikha, the tuft of hair a Brahmin usually ties atop his head, and took an oath to not tie it back until he dethroned Dhana Nanda.

The powerful pratigya (oath) taken by someone of the stature of Chanakya had its own spiritual power. Chanakya walked out of the court without looking back at the king. With this oath, the Nanda Empire's downfall was only a matter of time. Dhana Nanda would be the last king of the Nanda dynasty.

After returning from the court, Chanakya meditated. His anger had set events in motion and he now needed to heal his mind and focus on his goals. Alexander was the bigger threat and he needed a new plan to tackle him. Prioritizing his goals helped him understand the steps he needed to take immediately, and take stock of the feelings he had after being insulted in court.

When in anger, most of us do not know what to do. Chanakya had met Dhana Nanda face-to-face. He had controlled his anger, keeping in mind the larger goal. And then he had taken an oath to dethrone the king. It was important to recognize the urgency of one goal over another. *Protect Bharat, then dethrone Dhana Nanda.* Once the external threat was taken care of, he could execute the strategy he had in mind for the king.

He had set aside his personal enmity against Dhana Nanda in the face of a bigger problem. It was unfortunate that it amounted to no good. The need of the country is bigger than individual problems. When multiple challenges come to us simultaneously, we must keep ourselves calm. Then we need to decide which problem should be tackled first.

> We must never get impulsive and rush to solve all problems together. We will not be able to solve any problem in such a state of mind. When we tackle problems one at a time, one by one, all problems can be solved successfully.

This happens in wars as well. During a war, the enemy will try to attack us simultaneously from all directions. We need to understand the trick behind such a strategy. A good warrior understands the situation, analyses it and then prioritizes whom to attack first. This is the example of a strategic and tactical mind in action.

Dhana Nanda had refused to support Chanakya. Chanakya was determined not to let one king's refusal affect his plans. He approached other kings, and some joined his cause while others did not. In the end, the army that he managed to put together became larger in number than the one Alexander had. Using other strategies as well, such as employing the Vishkanyas, he defeated Alexander.

The external enemy was gone. Meanwhile, Chanakya had a new leader ready—his own student, Chandragupta Maurya, who had led the new group of allies against Alexander. Having witnessed his leadership capabilities, Chanakya was confident that Chandragupta would make a good emperor.

Chanakya's next goal was to dethrone Dhana Nanda. This became his priority. If Dhana Nanda was removed from the throne, there would be a vacuum at the top. It is always better to have a leader ready in waiting to fill in a vacancy. In Chandragupta, Chanakya had found the leader he needed.

There are three steps to creating a new leader, according to Chanakya:

1. Identify a potential leader.
2. Train that person.
3. Give him an opportunity.

Chanakya followed these guidelines with Chandragupta. He had identified his leadership potential long ago and had trained him in leadership skills. Having seen proof of his leadership qualities in the battle against Alexander, it was time to give Chandragupta the opportunity to ascend the throne of Magadh.

The only challenge remaining was that brilliant man—Amatya Rakshas. As long as Amatya was beside Dhana Nanda, it would be difficult to achieve what Chanakya had planned.

So what should be done in such a situation when the enemy also has an excellent minister? Such a strategy was not very easy to build. But Chanakya found a different method to handle this.

> The best wars are the ones that are won without fighting.

A neighbouring kingdom decided to wage war against Magadh. Chanakya used this opportunity to dethrone Dhana Nanda and bring in Chandragupta. When Amatya came to know about this, he figured out Chanakya's hand in it. Chanakya, however, did not kill Dhana Nanda. Defeating an enemy need not mean eliminating him. Dhana Nanda was exiled to the forest.

Chanakya advised him to live out the rest of his life there and contemplate on the wrongs he had done. Forgiveness is a trait in great men. Chanakya had won over his hatred towards Dhana Nanda.

When the guards took Dhana Nanda away, Chandragupta asked his teacher why he had spared the man's life. He felt that such a person could not be trusted to bow down in peace. Chanakya acknowledged Chandragupta's concerns and agreed that it was quite possible the crooked king would plot against them in the forest. He informed his protégé that he had instructed spies to keep an eye on the ousted king.

After Chandragupta was crowned the king of Magadh, Chanakya shifted his focus to the next goal— bringing Amatya Rakshas over to his side. The great scholar felt cheated and was furious with Chanakya for his plan which led to the defeat of Dhana Nanda. Chanakya approached the teacher with a request to continue in his position as the prime minister of Magadh and guide the new king to a prosperous future.

Outraged and defeated, Amatya felt insulted by this offer. Chanakya reminded the scholar that the whole world knew that in spite of having a bad ruler like Dhana Nanda, Magadh had remained the jewel of all kingdoms only because of him. He was the one responsible for keeping the government machinery running. Chanakya professed his reverence for the work done by Amatya and declared his support for him. He explained that Chandragupta was a young leader and would require wise advice from the senior minister. He requested Amatya to focus on the future of Magadh rather than dwell on the past of a defeated dynasty. The nation could continue to grow and prosper under Amatya's guidance.

Amatya was moved by Chanakya's humility and grace, and accepted the offer to continue as the prime minister. The golden days of Bharat had only started.

Meanwhile, Chanakya began to prepare for future wars. Instead of resting on his laurels after a new leader had taken charge, he started studying various scenarios of conflict in the future.

We will study those in the next chapter.

The more you sweat in peace, the less you bleed during war.

4

The Different Ways of War

> The king brings under his sway his own party as
> well as the party of the enemies, by the (use of the)
> treasury and the army.
>
> —*Arthashastra* (1.4.2)

When we think of war, what is the first thing that comes to our mind?

The battlefield, the soldiers, the machines, the gunshots, coupled with war cries and the cacophony of soldiers in pain. The tankers and fighter jets, bombs exploding all over, cities bombarded and thousands killed. To some extent, this may be a true image of war. But it is not the only kind of war.

There are different types of wars. Interestingly, one of them is the silent war, where there is neither noise, nor battlefield, nor weapons. It is all pure strategy.

Chanakya had classified war into three types:

1. Open war
2. Concealed war
3. Silent war

He knew that for different types of opponents, different methods had to be used.

Even with the best weapons and warriors at one's disposal, there is still no certainty of winning a war. Then what exactly gives one the edge? That elusive factor is the *strategy* behind the war.

Even the best warrior, in the most favourable circumstances, may not be able to guarantee victory. Therefore, we require a good strategist to aid the warriors. The brain is the strategist and the body is the warrior. When the brain and the body are in tune with each other, victory manifests.

We notice this in the Mahabharata. The best warrior among the Pandavas was Arjuna. He was not only a skilled archer, but also an able warrior. He was on the right side of dharma too. He had mastered all the techniques of warfare and there was no way he could lose.

Moreover, he was the best and favourite student of his teachers, Dronacharya and Kripacharya. If everything seemed right, what went wrong at the beginning even as the two armies faced each other?

The best warrior developed cold feet.

He could not think any further. Upon seeing the opponent, he started to lose his emotional balance. The opponents were none other than his relatives, teachers and friends. How could he fight against his own near and dear ones?

He decided not to fight.

Instead, he started to ponder: What is the use of winning a war by defeating our own people? What peace of mind would we have even if we won? Unable to reconcile himself to these conflicts, Arjuna decided to quit.

Then the greatest war strategist ever known in Indian history—Lord Krishna—came to Arjuna's rescue.

Arjuna had chosen him as his companion during the war. Krishna, though a king himself, had given his army to the opponent, Duryodhan, who was the leader of the Kauravas. Krishna was only to guide Arjuna and the Pandavas; he would not even lift a single weapon—that was the agreement.

Yet, Krishna's role as a strategist on the battlefield made all the difference. Initially, when Arjuna had chosen Krishna to be on his side, leaving the fully armed army to Duryodhan, it seemed like a bad choice. But the reality is: one good strategist on our side is better than millions of soldiers on the other side.

When Arjuna was totally lost and did not know what to do, Krishna played the most important role of giving him moral lessons on war. This dharma sankat, or ethical dilemma, that Arjuna was going through was resolved through a detailed discussion and deliberation between Arjuna and Krishna. This discussion and advice given by Krishna is contained in the Mahabharata as 700 Sanskrit shlokas, called the Bhagavadgita. It not only became a source of guidance and direction for Arjuna on the battlefield, it has remained a deep source of inspiration to everyone for generations to come. It is a venerated holy book among Hindus.

In fact, the Gita has been guiding everyone across the globe in finding answers to moral dilemmas at every stage of life. Life's battles can be won if we understand the principles given in the Gita.

Krishna laughs at Arjuna and calls him a fool for getting carried away and forgetting his role as a warrior, for external reasons. Later, when all the questions that plagued him had been answered by Krishna, Arjuna stood up, ready to fight. The role of Krishna on the battlefield was not just to make Arjuna rise and fight. That was just the beginning. The next step was to guide him through every move that was required to defeat the enemy.

The role of Krishna as a strategist has to be studied if one has to understand Chanakya fully. Because Chanakya had also learned from Krishna and other warfare exerts from the Mahabharata. This finds mention in *Kautilya's Arthashastra* that Chanakya wrote based on his study of various gurus who taught war methods.

Krishna was a strategist, and so was Chanakya. Both of them were advisors who acted as catalysts. They were outside the war, yet an intrinsic part of it. While Krishna directed Arjuna, Chanakya advised Chandragupta. And their advice brought victory on all battlefields.

As the saying goes, 'Advisors can make you or break you. Therefore choose your advisors carefully.'

Once we have the right advisors on our side, we need to make sure we implement the ideas they have given us.

Now we will look at the three different types of wars according to Chanakya:

1. Open war

This is usually the most well-known type of war. Open war is described as the war fought between states. When two kingdoms go to war directly by crossing each other's borders, we call that an open war. The soldiers are on the fields, attacking each other. There is open combat and the enemy is right in front of us.

In an open war, everything happens right in front of our eyes. Sometimes, some leaders or kings use a psychological strategy in open war by challenging the opponent to surrender by showing the strength of the army.

Usually, when the enemy approaches with full force, the king under attack would always prefer to avoid facing it. So the aggressor has a strategic advantage. He declares, 'You better surrender or I will destroy you.' In such a case, a weak king will surrender easily.

But open war is not just about the attack. It should also be about strategy. The right thing to do in case of an open war is to think through all the dimensions first. One may be weaker than the opponent, but one needs to think carefully to see if there is something one can do in the given circumstances.

Therefore, Chanakya says that even in the most difficult situations or in an emergency, such a king should call his ministers and advisors, and ask them what is to be done. Even in the most hopeless of situations, there is often a way out. In the old days, the kings would call a meeting and ask everyone their opinion and also examine all the available options. The king would abide by what the majority declared, or what was most conducive to the situation.

Remember, in a war, there are many rights and wrongs. Sitting and deliberating with experts might enable us to get some breakthrough ideas. War should never be an impulsive decision. It should always be thought through.

Similarly, the king who has declared war by attacking should not be impulsive. Being surrounded by experts and asking their opinion is always the best way to tackle an open war.

In the Ramayana, Rama, along with the vanara sena, or the army of monkeys, was going to attack Ravana, who had kidnapped Rama's consort, Sita. Everyone was ready for an open war. But Rama had the wisdom to think before attacking.

He held a meeting with the experts in the group. Sugreeva, his friend in the battle, had a wise person named Jambavan in his council. Jambavan suggested that instead of a direct attack, they should send a spy to know more about the situation on the ground. It was possible that Sita was not in Lanka. Perhaps, she had been shifted to a different place. Or it could well be that she had already escaped from Lanka. It was always better to verify the facts before an open war.

That is when Jambavan decided to send Hanuman to Lanka to carry out a reality check. This would not only assure them of Sita's presence in Lanka, but also help them study and understand the conditions at play in Lanka.

Hanuman was not just physically powerful, capable of flying to Lanka and back. He was also well-versed in the scriptures. He was intelligent and had a mind of his own. He was also well-equipped with decision-making powers. On enemy territory, depending on the situation, one must use one's discretion in all actions. There is a high risk of being captured by the enemy and the spy can be tortured and put to death.

Hanuman seemed to be the best fit for such an eventuality. So when he went to Lanka, he collected all the information required for the war first-hand. He checked if Sita was there, had a discussion with her, and informed her that Rama was coming to rescue her. He met Ravana and warned him about the forthcoming attack. He also advised him that to avoid the war, he should release Sita.

Others in Ravana's court wondered that if the envoy of Rama, Hanuman, could be so powerful as to destroy Lanka, imagine the power of Rama himself. This is an example of the kind of message that can be conveyed by an envoy, or in modern-day terms, the sort of dialogue that can be initiated to broker peace, before an open war actually begins.

Not only did he warn the enemy before the war started, but while in the enemy kingdom, Hanuman also understood who were the ones supporting Rama's cause. Vibhishan was a devotee of Lord Rama even though he was the brother of Ravana. When Hanuman and Vibhishan met, they discussed Rama. Vibhishan also warned Ravana against the war. But Ravana did not listen to the advice of his wise brother.

While on the other side, Rama, who paid heed to the advice of elders and experts such as Jambavan, won the battle.

Another important aspect of discussion is consultation with the women contingent. Their power, inputs and insights are essential, according to Chanakya.

It is usually believed that war is a man's game. That may be true to some extent, but the impact of a war is felt not just on men. Women, who are an equal part of any society, are equally affected. Therefore, Chanakya suggested a discussion with the women in the kingdom before the war took place.

The king would usually discuss the matter with his wife (raja patni) and his mother (raja mata). These two were the most powerful women in the kingdom and also represented two different generations. These royal ladies would get an input from other ladies too through their network. If a kingdom had to go to war, the women were also informed. This ensured that they were better prepared to handle the tough days of the war.

There are several methods of preparing for open war before every warrior goes for the final attack. One of the prominent methods is: 'Your best warrior against mine.'

In this method, both the armies are face-to-face. The kings go for a duel. They call for their best warriors. And only these two warriors fight each other. They represent the whole army. So whichever warrior wins, the army he represents wins. The defeated warrior's army has to surrender to the winner. The winner takes it all. In many cases, the kings are the best warriors on each side.

There are many advantages to this method. Many lives are saved. The war is not prolonged and victory or defeat is a matter of time. When the best warrior is fighting, she/he knows that they have to give their best for the kingdom. And then the better of the two wins.

But after all this, if nothing works, open war is declared. All the soldiers march forth. The enemy tries to protect itself from every possible move. Ammunitions and weapons are put to use. All the warriors give their best.

2. Concealed war

The second form of war is concealed war. This is similar to guerrilla warfare. A small group of people, sometimes a single person, fights against a larger troop. Here, the size does not matter. It's the strategy that counts the most.

In guerrilla warfare, a small group is the best bet. The ability to move quickly and fast makes the difference. The moves are strategic in nature. They are so sudden that the enemy is often taken by surprise. Operations are carried out in a secretive manner. It is not the power of weapons but the power of the mind that accounts for everything.

Shivaji, the great Maratha king and the founder of the Maratha Empire, was known to use this strategy a lot. His method was compared to thunder and lightning, striking the opponent when least expected. He did not have the best of armies, nor did he have the best of weapons. He had an army of young, tribal boys and men, and yet, what made all the difference were his methods of strategic attacks.

His killing of Afzal Khan was strategic in approach. He had an opportunity to come face-to-face with him. Afzal khan was tall and huge and this gave him an advantage over Shivaji. But Shivaji killed his opponent using the claws of a tiger, tearing open his belly. An important part of concealed war is knowing what move to make and when.

We find that Shivaji used the strategy of concealed warfare in capturing various forts in the region. Shivaji lived for barely fifty years, but what he accomplished during his lifetime is impossible for many warriors put together. He was the founder of an impressive empire that spread across India. The Maratha Empire had nearly 400 forts. He built some of them. But the others were strategically captured by him.

The warfare strategies given in the *Arthashastra* were applied in the life of Shivaji. Military experts have drawn parallels between what the *Arthashastra* preaches and what Shivaji practised. He did study the *Arthashastra*, and his guru Swami Ramdas guided him in various military strategies as well.

Even before Shivaji, we find many examples of forts being constructed in the region using inputs from the *Arthashastra*. One of them is the Daulatabad fort near Aurangabad, which is also acclaimed as one of the best forts in India, having many strategic advantages for a concealed war. It has seven doors, each of them constructed strategically. It was practically impossible for any enemy to enter the fort undetected. Even if they did, they would get lost in the maze it was and be easy fodder for the soldiers inside.

Such strategies were used by Chanakya. But then only a deeper study and understanding of military science will help us to decode all the secrets Chanakya used.

Hopefully, you, my reader, will find yourself interested in military science and study the subject. Great kings have used these strategies and prevailed over their enemies for thousands of years.

3. Silent war

A silent war is not fought on the battlefield. It does not usually have an external enemy, and it is fought on a continued basis inside the kingdom, so that the power of the enemy king is diluted slowly and steadily.

In the *Arthashastra*, Chanakya mentions various types of internal, silent wars one can fight. This usually begins by sowing seeds of dissatisfaction among the subjects. The whole operation is strategic in nature. The only difference between concealed and silent warfare is that military action is very minimal in the latter. Though there is military intervention, it is not visible at the surface level.

One of the best ways to fight a silent war is to use the spying and espionage system. Spies are always gathering information. After piecing these together, the king, along with his ministers, forms a plan. They prepare a strategy to see what can disrupt the opponent.

An in-depth knowledge of psychology—both individual and social—is necessary for this process. For example, it is commonly believed that people in power are always afraid of losing their power. And also that people around powerful people want to grow more powerful.

So, using this psychological factor, Chanakya would devise the strategy of a power game between the king and his ministers. The king's family, too, would be a part of this power struggle.

A king's brothers and cousins may not be happy with the king's powers. Then, there are the children of the king and their cousins. They engage in their own internal power struggle. The successor to the throne is always eager to ascend it as early as possible.

This understanding of the psychological power game can be used as a strategy against any opponent. The solution in the above case is to start preparing the potential successor early on. Some ministers, too, try to instigate an internal war among the king's family members as a competition for the throne. This automatically causes a rift, and a silent war ensues.

This is very close to *Bheda* in the four-fold strategy of Chanakya. The king has to look at such situations from a long-term perspective. He may even need to fund the operations for a long period of time.

When we study the two world wars, we find a similar approach, where spies worked furtively in the enemy country to trigger a silent war. This was also the case in the 'cold war'. There was no direct attack. Yet, there was a war taking place, and sometimes, it took lives. There is something unusual about a silent war. It may be unfolding around us, but we wouldn't know.

And even if we have an inkling of it, we would not be able to do much about it. By the time we grasped the situation and made an attempt to solve the problem, it would probably be too late. It is like a termite attack. One notices that the wood is becoming weak even if it looks strong on the outside. The termite is rendering the wood hollow *from within*.

That is the key in a silent war. It all happens within the kingdom, within an organization. By the time one gets wind of it, the damage is done. We may remove one affected log of wood and replace it with a new piece, but the other pieces have been already affected. The whole house is jeopardized. The roof may just cave in before we can even think of remedial measures. The question then, upon investigation, is how did the termite get to the wood? Was it always there, dormant? Was it introduced by someone? Was there an oversight while building the house? It may be that it has been there for a long time, working away slowly, silently and steadily. There was no direct, sudden attack.

Even today, if you look around the globe, such silent wars are taking place. No government authority can do much about it. Look at the drug mafia. They are active in all major cities of the world. Everyone is aware of it, yet little can be done to address it. The media may not be able to decode it either. And one day, suddenly, it comes to the surface. A whole generation of boys and girls would have succumbed to drugs. It takes a prolonged effort to recover from the mess. It may even take a few generations to fight this kind of war.

Chanakya had a deeper understanding of such situations at a social level. Therefore, while writing the *Arthashastra*, he also proposed studying *samaj shastra* (social sciences). Understanding how society works is an important part of war strategy. This is where social psychology works. To prevail over the enemy, Chanakya advised silent war. He propounded on various methods to avoid becoming a victim of a silent war.

Many economic, religious, traditional and cultural strategies are used. Once emotional aspects come into play, there is a chance that people will slowly turn against the government or establishment. These anti-establishment moves are often planted against the ruler by the enemy king. When we look at these different types of wars, we find that there are several calculations involved in fighting the enemy.

Now that we have seen and discussed the different types of war, here is the million-dollar question: *Which type of war do we use against the enemy?*

The answer is: it depends on the type of enemy and situation one is confronted with. As we know, one measure does not fit all. A tailor knows that every person is different and so is their body structure. The same person can gain or lose weight from time to time. So, a good tailor understands that stitching a perfect dress involves customization.

Similarly in war, we need to assess the situation and work out the strategy. What worked in the past may not guarantee success now. Military experts know that. So did Chanakya. If a battle was won in the past using a particular strategy, there is no guarantee that it will work in the current situation.

The enemy may have got better with their strategy and learnt from their failures. They may have new weapons. The number of soldiers in their camp may have increased, and the army general may have changed. The battlefield may have moved to a different location. One needs to look at all these aspects before actually selecting the type of war one will use.

> We need not choose only one type of warfare to attack our enemy. It can be a combination of all of them.

This is where wisdom comes in. A wise person knows what to pick up and when, and does the needful. Ultimately, results matter. Such a person is a true strategist. According to Chanakya, any person using aanvikshiki is bound to win whatever the circumstance. We must think about every dimension before going to war. One well thought-out move is far better and more effective than a hundred hasty ones. We must aim at making our move perfect.

It is all in the mind. We need to prepare our mind first, and then plan our attack. A calm and composed mind is the best weapon in any war.

The last but most important point to remember and understand is that there are different types of opponents. There are different kinds of kings. One should choose the type of war depending on the king or the opponent.

Let us read on to know how Chanakya faced one such situation in Magadh.

* * *

One day, Chanakya came to know that a neighbouring king was planning to attack Magadh.

Magadh was the strongest kingdom in the country and it was impossible to defeat it. It had the largest army, and with Chandragupta as its king and an advisor like Chanakya, who would dare attack it?

In the past, one of the neighbouring kings had tried and had failed miserably. It had been akin to a fight between the elephant and the ant. When Chanakya heard that the neighbouring king was again planning to attack the mighty kingdom of Magadh, he sent out his spies to gather more information. The spies came back with a smile.

'The enemy is being stupid as always. They have tried to attack us in the past and lost. We have studied them again and found that there has been practically no change in their might. The size of the army and the number of soldiers are still the same. The king is same. The weapons and ammunition too. So what worked in the past will surely work for us in the present too.'

Chanakya smiled and said, 'Think again. Try to see if you are missing anything. And only after that will we decide what we need to choose as our strategy for war against this small enemy.'

The spies went back and tried to gather more information about the opponent. But they could not find anything different from what they had seen earlier. Reporting back to Chanakya, the spies did not have any new inputs. Earlier, they had tried the open war strategy, and they thought that the same would work this time too.

'We will use the silent method this time,' said Chanakya.

Everyone was surprised. Why use a long-term strategy of silent war when the enemy is weak and can be finished off immediately?

'Why, Acharya? The power of the neighbouring king is the same. We were successful with an open war strategy the last time. Why change now?'

Well-informed and astute strategist that he was, Chanakya said, 'Just recently, the king married a princess and made her his new queen. She is the daughter of a powerful king. With that, his strength has increased manifold.'

That set the people present thinking.

'When a king marries and has a new queen, the kingdom gains in strength. Now, even without expanding his own army, he has a bigger army on his side. His father-in-law's kingdom automatically becomes an ally. This doubles his power.'

He concluded, 'Instead of a quick open fight, we need to attack the enemy silently this time. I have to use the termite method. Render them hollow from within.'

That is called wisdom in war.

Whatever is necessary for the situation should be applied appropriately.

5

Sama, Dana, Danda, Bheda—
the four-fold strategy

He should win over those of them who are friendly
with conciliation and gifts, those hostile through
dissensions and force.

—*Arthashastra* (11.1.3)

One day, Chanakya was sitting quietly in deep thought
when Chandragupta came to meet him at the gurukul.
Chanakya had played a vital role in making Chandragupta
the king and was happy that Amatya Rakshas had agreed
to continue being advisor to him.

Chandragupta used to meet his guru once every week
to discuss the problems he encountered in running the
kingdom. Chanakya believed in the king and by pointing

him in the right direction with relevant reminders from his studies, he would help Chandragupta find solutions on his own.

The king waited outside his guru's kutia. After a while, when Chanakya noticed that Chandragupta had arrived, he called him inside.

He apologized to the king for keeping him waiting and informed him that he had been engrossed in his thoughts. Chandragupta, a student at heart, enquired about what it was that was distracting his guru.

Chanakya replied in a tone of banter that the king would have to keep pace with the speed of his mind to understand what it meant. When Chandragupta humbly asked his guru to try his hand, Chanakya gave him the following pointers, which are applicable and valuable even today for all leaders:

- The biggest strategy is the one that remains in the mind. If everyone knows about it, it is not a strategy at all.
- Mystery is the biggest asset of a great strategist. All leaders have to understand that they live in two worlds at the same time—one is known to others, while the other should always be kept separate from the team or subjects.
- As a good leader, one should remember that there are certain secrets that others, not just competitors

but also team members, or, as in Chandragupta's case, his subjects, should never know.

- One should never trust one's subjects or team members blindly. One needs to determine who can be trusted with important information. It is a possibility that competitors, or in Chandragupta's case, his enemies, might have spies who might prey on his innocent subjects for information.

Chanakya advised the king to work on developing *vivek buddhi*, the power of discrimination, which comes with experience. Learning is a lifelong process, while relearning is a step towards perfection. Chanakya asked the king to stay back and attend his afternoon lecture on a new topic under war strategy—the method of Sama, Dana, Danda, Bheda. Chandragupta had enjoyed learning about this at the gurukul.

One can play around with those four magic words. The permutations and combinations of those words contain infinite possibilities. They are like notes of music. A good musician would make use of the same notes as others, but bring out a new melody every time.

* * *

In the *Arthashastra*, Chanakya has written extensively about this four-fold policy used against enemies.

Sama means discussion. Whenever a problem needs to be solved, open discussions with the parties involved.

Dana entails solving the problem financially. There is always an economic angle to solving every problem. Try and explore that.

Danda means punishment. We need to attack the opponent, if required. It is important to show our might so that the enemy does not take us for granted.

Bheda implies creating a divide. Engineering internal divisions in the enemy camp is a tried-and-tested way of winning a war.

It is not easy to understand the power of these words. They can make or break a kingdom. Therefore, the king or leader has to be extra careful of certain facts while using these ideas.

- We should never take the enemy (read competition) for granted. They may be using the same ideas as we are. We must try to figure out the intentions and plans of the competition and keep our strategy a secret.
- War, or any challenge, is often just a mind game. One who understands the mind of the opponent wins the game. One has to be vigilant and alert.
- When the battle begins, there is no time to think. We have a strategic advantage if we have thought out our plans in advance.

Let us now study the four terms in detail and understand their application in the real world.

Sama

In his lecture, Chanakya went on to explain the negative aspects of war:

'War is not good. It destroys many things. What took generations to create can be undone in one day of war.

'Big monuments which represent civilization are uprooted. People die, women are raped, children slaughtered. Money is looted from homes and temples. Moreover, the loss goes beyond what is visible—it has a psychological impact as well, resulting in stress.

'War affects many generations to come. Children born in war-torn countries go through a lot of mental agony. They seldom recover from the pain of what they saw as children, the death and bloodshed all around. These images are permanently imprinted on their minds and become a part of their lives.'

Conjuring the many horrors of war, Chanakya continued, 'And one should see the place where a war has taken place. Dead bodies do not get cremated. They rot as if they were not human beings at all. Finally, even if they are cremated, these are mass cremations, where most of the bodies are not even identified. Many families never see the bodies of the departed ones.

'And after the war, if the new ruler is not good, the torture continues. The warriors' widows become slaves and prostitutes. There is no dignity for those who are left alive. They pray for deliverance; they would rather have died. Because even though they are alive, they are as good as dead.

'The aged do not know what to do. They can't fight back due to lack of physical strength. They have lost the houses and wealth that they created. It is better to die a rich man than be looted by others and die destitute.

'And finally, people migrate or run away to far-off places. Even for those who are alive and flee, there is no hope. They need to find new friends, new jobs in a new place. They are not easily accepted. They are considered refugees begging for survival. They are not respected and lose their dignity and honour. It will take a few generations for them to integrate themselves with the new region, if at all. Till then, such a person will be considered a second-grade citizen.'

When all this was explained, the students learnt that, as leaders, one should think a thousand times before going to war with anyone. Giving everyone some time to ponder over his teachings, Chanakya offered an alternative.

'Therefore, the first step in war is to avoid war itself. This is one of the easiest ways to defeat your enemy. Why fight a war if the demands and concerns can be addressed over discussions? One of the most important reasons why wars happen is misunderstanding. Once we sit down with a cool head and discuss things, we can avoid the any war . . .

'The Sanskrit term "sama" has many meanings . . . thinking with equanimity . . . a steady mind. It also implies equality and respect, discussion and problem-solving.

'So when a problem arises, you should not jump to conclusions. It is better to deal with the problem with a quiet and composed mind. It is important that we should never "react" to an enemy, but instead, "respond".

'A reaction is often impulsive, it lacks deliberation. We feel we are right and the other person is wrong, and our decision is not thought through. Whereas, when we respond, we take time doing so. We analyse and take into consideration every aspect of the problem. We consider the possibility that the opponent could also be right.'

The students were then taken through the process of using sama in warfare.

'Whenever you think of going to war, curb the impulse. It is possible that as a king you want to demonstrate your power. Your ego will surface and tell you to declare war immediately. But then you have to stop that urge. You will have to call upon the council of ministers. Yes, this is the first step in practising sama: call your ministers and hold a meeting. These minsters are your advisors. Never take a decision without discussing the same with experts. Your ministers are your sounding board, they are mature and experienced people and they know what is good for the kingdom.'

He then went on to define the qualities of a minister.

'A good council of ministers will give you not just one view, but also a counterview. They may ask you difficult questions. They will then tell you what can be done. They will help you look at the situation objectively. And when the ministers help you think, you should think along with them.'

With a smile, Chanakya continued, 'The worst thing to do is to think alone. Why not take the help of another person's thinking faculty? After all, your ministers are intelligent people. You should use their intellect along with your own. This will give you a perspective that thinking alone will never give. Think together and think different.'

Then the teacher outlined the next step of action.

'Ask for a meeting with the enemy. Yes, never meet an enemy straightaway on the battlefield. You should try to arrange a meeting with the leader of the enemy first.'

A student spoke up. 'Acharya, what if the enemy king does not want to meet us? What if he is not ready for a discussion?'

Chanakya liked the question. It was thought-provoking.

'Yes, you have a point there,' he replied. 'It is possible that the other king may not give you an audience. In such a scenario, you have two options before you. First, write a letter. When you put down what you want to say in writing, the other party will at least read it. And you can express many things better in writing than you would do face-to-face. Second, send an envoy. Your envoy is your representative. And the rules of raja niti say that an envoy, even from the enemy, is to be respected. He is often called the "shanti doot", or messenger of peace. The envoy is not going to war. He is someone who wants to solve the problem.'

Chanakya explained the rules regarding deploying an envoy. This is explained in detail in a chapter titled 'Vidyasamuddeshah' in Book 1 of the *Arthashastra*.

He then went on to narrate a Puranic story, one that is often recalled in Indian culture.

'Remember Hanuman going to Lanka to meet Ravana. Ravana had kidnapped Sita. The objective was to release Sita. The army of monkeys was ready to attack the enemy. But Jambavan, senior advisor to Sugreeva, instructed Hanuman to go to Lanka first, before the whole army landed there.'

Chanakya next expounded on some of the stories and war strategies in the Ramayana.

'Hanuman going to Lanka before the army launched an attack had two objectives. First, he wanted to make sure that Sita was present in Lanka, ascertain that the enemy had not shifted her to a different place. It was important to send someone to verify this. Second, he went as an envoy, a shanti doot. A meeting took place between Hanuman and Ravana in Lanka.

'Ravana asked him, "Who are you?"

'Hanuman replied, "I am Rama's doot, the messenger of Lord Rama." Hanuman explained that he did not have any personal agenda. That he had come as a representative of Rama and his role was to convey the message of peace.'

The entire scene came alive in the eyes of the students.

'Hanuman told Ravana, "Why go to war? Just return Sita. That is all that is required. And all of us will be in peace."

'But the arrogant Ravana did not listen. He did not use his thinking faculties. He was so full of false pride and ego that he did not foresee the consequences of the impending war. He had good advisors, including Vibhishan. His own wife, Mandodari, suggested that he return Sita to Rama. But Ravana stuck to what he believed was right. This is where ego plays a role before an actual war starts . . .'

After a contemplative pause, Chanakya continued, 'Hanuman had met Sita in Lanka and made sure she was there. Once he came back, the requisite steps were taken to go to Lanka . . .

This is how Chanakya explained the concept of sama to his students, using examples and analysing the same. He paused to take a few deep breaths, giving the students a break to reflect on what they had been told. After a while, he resumed his lecture.

'Now, I will continue with the next strategy—dana.'

Dana

This method was close to Chanakya's heart. As a strategist, he knew this method worked well with most people.

'Dana involves solving the problem using financial means.'

Chanakya was an expert in arthashastra—also known as the science of economics. So he knew that money matters count the most. He understood its psychological aspect. He knew that money could influence most people in the world—the strong and the weak, the rich and the poor. The power of money could solve a lot of problems.

'In this world, there is no one who does not understand the value of money. Right from a pauper to a prince, everyone is connected through money. The poor man may require money to survive. While the rich might need it to solve more complicated problems. Money can also be a powerful tool to demonstrate one's clout to others.'

The teacher expounded in simple terms what we call microeconomics and macroeconomics.

'Drops of water make up the ocean. Some people understand the drops, while others are interested in the ocean. The common man might use every drop that comes his way whereas kings and powerful people delve into the ocean. One should be able to see the relationship between the drops and the ocean. Both the drop and the ocean are water after all. Only the scale differs. The intelligent person will see water as a common element in the drop and the ocean.

'A strategist always looks for connections. He looks for commonalities and patterns. Money, as we know, has many facets to it. What connects everyone in this world is happiness. Everyone wants to be happy. And money makes everyone happy. That is why our currency is called "mudra". Mudra means that which gives happiness.'

* * *

During his time, Chanakya had defined the complete economic system for the Magadh Empire. And mudra was the currency of exchange. He had even developed a highly evolved coinage system. It had gold, silver and copper coins. These were called mudras.

Goods would be sold in exchange for coins, or mudras. Chanakya went beyond the barter system in which goods were exchanged for goods. He believed that the value of a thing or a person also needed to be measured. And the measure of a thing, or the worth of a person, should be decided by paying the right amount of money.

* * *

Chanakya told his students, 'When you respect a person, pay him the right amount of money. That is why when it is time to go, pay dakshina, give the right quantity, as per your capacity.'

The students immediately understood the meaning of gurudakshina. They realized that when they completed their education, they should pay the guru as per their capacity, but they also needed to value the education they had received.

Coming back to the topic of war, Chanakya explained the concept of money as a solution in war.

'The second strategy—dana—can be used to avoid war. When sama, that is discussion, fails to give results, try this strategy. When we talk to the enemy in economic terms, they might see reason.'

Examining one of the key reasons behind war, he continued, 'War happens for economic reasons too;

there are economic wars as well. When an enemy attacks, he loots the treasury. That is why Alexander attacked Bharatvarsha. The Greek king wanted to expand his kingdom. But he also knew that Bharat was proverbial golden bird. So if he defeated us, he would grow richer.'

Looking at Chandragupta, Chanakya went on, 'We created an army that was powerful enough to defeat Alexander. Or else, he would have taken away all the wealth from this country. We would have been poor and starving by now. So, never let the enemy deprive you of your wealth.'

At the same time, Chanakya was not against exchange of wealth with other nations and he elaborated on this aspect.

'We need to keep trade relations with others. Countries are dependent on each other through trading. There should be a constant exchange of goods. This is healthy for every nation. What is produced in one country should be sold in others. And we should obtain through trade what is good in other nations. Such trade binds the human race together. Leaders should understand traders. These traders can help us avoid wars.'

This was a new dimension that Chanakya brought into the discussion.

'Yes, traders and merchants are important in order to avoid wars. They are no ordinary people. They have so much understanding of money matters that they can be used as war strategists.'

'When the political envoy, the shanti doot, is not able to resolve matters with the enemy king, try sending a trade delegation.'

This was a powerful dimension that the students had not thought about.

'Wealth is energizing. Talking in terms of monetary gains invigorates the other party. Who does not like economic benefits?'

The students, too, suddenly felt energetic talking about money.

'This is the concept of dana. Try it out to avoid wars. Because, when it comes to wars, if you reveal the economic aspect, the other party might also be motivated to avoid the war. It works in most cases . . .

Chanakya's eyes blazed with anger as he spoke the next words.

'But some enemies are stupid. They understand neither sama nor dana. They need to be dealt with differently. They only understand—danda.'

Danda

Giving the analogy of a child, Chanakya explained, 'Danda means punishment. When a child does not understand something said with love, you need to punish him. The punishment will set things right. If not punished, the child will grow arrogant and a time will come when it will be too late for him to mend his ways.'

He explained the need for punishment.

'Punishment is necessary. But one should understand the right amount of punishment. If employed in excess, you will become a terror. If you do not punish at all, the enemy will take you for granted. The right amount of punishment will give you honour and respect.'

Chanakya delved into the theory of punishment in greater detail.

'Using war strategies is also called danda niti. The strategy used to punish the enemy is danda niti. This is a carefully thought through policy if we need to actually go for the attack. Even though we should try and avoid war, there are times when it becomes necessary. War results in destruction. However, if we do not show the enemy our power on the battlefield, it can lead to more destruction.'

Chanakya had built a powerful army against Alexander. He knew that if he had not wielded his power, Alexander would easily have destroyed the whole nation.

'Power respects power. If we are not powerful, the enemy will take us for granted. Sometimes, it is essential to demonstrate your power through war. Military power has to be used. But one has to ensure it is not misused.

And one who knows how to use his might against the enemy is a true leader. Let the enemy know that you are ready for war if required so that it thinks twice before embarking on that path. We have to send out the message that if they want to destroy us, we know how to destroy them as well.'

At this point, Chanakya got into the history of wars.

'Powerful kings know that we should be ready to die on the battlefield if the honour and respect of the nation is at stake. To be ready to attack shows that you have dignity and self-respect. So take up the challenge of going into war when required. Call your ministers and army generals. Call the war experts. Call the women too. Call the elders. And then taking their suggestions and blessings, get ready to march on to the battlefield.'

In a voice that conveyed that now there was no looking back, Chanakya continued.

'You should have the best of weapons. The best of strategies. The most powerful and motivated soldiers. Then, when you go to war, there is no reason why you should not win the war. Wars are to be avoided, yes. But if that's not an option, wars have to be won. It would be stupid to go to war and lose. So plan well before you attack. And once you attack, go for the kill. Your arrow should not miss the target. Your sword should sever the head from the shoulder at first blow, leave an immediate mark on the enemy's psyche.

'Warriors are not seen on the battlefield. They stand fully prepared for a long time before they go into war. They are the ones who are ready to charge at any moment. So that when the right time comes, they can finish off the enemy.'

The air was charged with a sense of power as Chanakya expounded on the concept of danda.

An intelligent student posed a question.

'Acharya, what if we are not as powerful as the enemy. What if they have a bigger army? Better warriors and weapons.'

The acharya then put forth the fourth strategy.

'Then we use bheda.'

Bheda

Bheda means divide. This is a strategy that never fails. A smaller king can easily defeat a powerful and bigger enemy using this method.

'Bheda entails splitting the enemy within itself. It is called the dual policy.'

Chanakya now began explaining power from a different dimension.

'The power of the enemy lies in its unity. When everyone in the enemy camp stands united and together, it is not easy to defeat them. But, if split from within, the most powerful enemy will fight amongst themselves.

Divided, they lose all the power they have. You do not have to kill the enemy. Let them kill themselves. It is a policy of divide and rule. Let them divide themselves, and you rule.'

Chanakya went on to summarize the four-fold strategies.

'Sometimes, what works with one enemy may not work with another. So you should reflect on which strategy works with which opponent. The right timing matters too. The right strategy executed at the wrong time will is doomed to fail.

'Also crucial is the right place. If you call the enemy to your place, you have a strategic advantage in sama. If you give more economic benefits to the opponent than they expect, it could work to your advantage. And a surprise danda or attack will catch the enemy by surprise . . .

'And yes, never let the enemy know that you are planning the divide-and-win policy within their own people.'

The class was coming to an end. But the students had only just been introduced to a great concept they would practise lifelong.

While for the young students of the gurukul, this was a new concept, for Chandragupta, it amounted to revising what he had learned earlier.

After closing prayers, the class was dismissed.

Chanakya and Chandragupta walked out of the class together. Both were silent and reflective.

After a few moments, the teacher told the student, 'Chandragupta, next time you come, do take a class yourself with these young students. We have practised sama, dana, danda and bheda in our various battles. Share your experiences with them. They will benefit from listening to your side of the story, your experiences . . .'

Excited about the prospect of teaching young minds, the king replied, 'Yes, Acharya, it will be a privilege. I look forward to it.'

Chanakya then addressed his most capable student in a commanding tone, as if issuing an order.

'But for now, go back. You need to rule the kingdom too. That is what you are supposed to do first. I will do the teaching, you do the ruling.'

Both of them had a hearty laugh as Chanakya disappeared into his kutia while Chandragupta made his way to his palace, both determined to do their respective duties to protect the country from external and internal enemies.

6

War as a Game of Chess

After ascertaining the relative strength or weakness of powers, place, time, revolts in rear, losses, expenses, gains and troubles, of himself and of the enemy, the conqueror should march.

—*Arthashastra* (9.1.1)

Chanakya always encouraged his students to play games. He taught them both physical and mental games. If we study the daily routine of a king, we will find that there is enough time for him to engage in varied kinds of activities. Physical activities include exercises, walks, inspection of the military, hunting, and so on. Mental activities include strategic thinking, discussions with experts and study.

One of the best ways to develop our intellect is to play games that are stimulating. Such games force us to think and come up with breakthrough solutions to problems. One has to be alert not only while preparing for or during war, but even after it, during times of peace. Even after the war has been won, Chanakya would not allow the king to relax. A leader has to be ever vigilant. He wanted a leader who was physically strong and mentally alert to be at the helm of the kingdom.

The tables could always turn even from a winning position. We must never take victory for granted because, the moment that happens, the enemy will take over. Therefore, it is essential not to relax before or after war times.

One of the best ways of being prepared for war is to keep thinking about it.

There is a famous story about a coach who spoke about the 'rule of 24' and urged his players to follow it. Winning and losing are natural outcomes of any game. But be it victory or loss, a good sportsman should always be ready for the next game.

What is the rule of 24?

This rule states that whatever the result, one should take a break of twenty-four hours after the game. So, .in case we win a game, it is worth celebrating the win for twenty-four hours after the game. However, even if we are defeated, the twenty-four hours after are vital to help settle and calm our negative emotions. We can analyse and think through why we lost, in what aspect was the opponent better, what we could have done differently.

The rule of 24 states that, be it success or failure, victory or loss, we should take a break only for one day. Then we must get back to the field to start all over again. We should not sit back and relax beyond that. We should be ready for the field in twenty-four hours.

The same rule goes for warriors too. The leader of an army or the king should never let success make him complacent or defeat render him despondent.

Practice is key.

The best army keeps itself fit, physically and mentally, perpetually. It engages in mock drills and practises war strategies.

But our focus here is the mental and intellectual fitness required in war strategy. One needs to be alert in war, and to do that, one has to make it a habit. And, in doing that, the most important factor is practice.

One of the methods to keep ourselves intellectually active is to imagine and practise various warfare scenarios, visualize moves that the enemy might make. And then to plan potential countermoves. In modern-day military warfare, there are various such techniques available. There are simulators and mock drills, military exercises and war games. In fact, two or more countries could collaborate on war games for better training.

* * *

One day, Chanakya was deeply engrossed in studying. After contemplating war strategies for some time, he decided that he wanted to meet Chandragupta. He sent a messenger to check on the king of Magadh, so they could meet and talk about potential enemy attacks.

The messenger returned to tell Chanakya that Chandragupta was busy playing chaturanga. He also informed the teacher that he had gone to the extent of informing the ministers that games such as chaturanga should not be prioritized over meeting one's guru.

To the messenger's surprise, though, Chanakya gave a satisfied look and told him that he was happy with the king's choice as he himself had advised Chandragupta to play chaturanga in order to become an expert in war strategies.

Chaturanga

In Sanskrit, 'chatur' means four and 'anga' means parts. Chaturanga is a board game that kings played in earlier times. Akin to modern games designed to understand strategies, chaturanga was popular back then.

In chaturanga, as the name suggests, an army had four parts—chariots, horses, elephants and soldiers.

In the armies of the era, kings and senior commanders would be in chariots controlled by charioteers. These chariots stocked weapons for the commanders' use. During a war, the charioteers would navigate to strategic locations, while the commander would focus solely on the target.

The Mahabharata is a great example of why a good commander-charioteer combination is vital. Lord Krishna was the charioteer, while Arjuna was the warrior. Lord Krishna constantly advised Arjuna on war moves and weapons to be used specific to a situation.

Another big advantage of this combined effort is that there are two minds working together. Having a good charioteer was a strategic advantage to the commanders. Commanders made sure they had the best charioteers on their side.

Next came the horses. In those days, kings were trained to be good at horse-riding. This was important for a warrior. It allowed the rider to pierce through the enemy and launch quick attacks. Taming a wild horse was a test for a good warrior as it forged a relationship between the horse and its master that proved invaluable in wars. Be it Shivaji or Rana Pratap, all the great war heroes of our land were also great horsemen.

Even today, horse-riding is taught in a few military schools and the armed forces. The Sardar Patel Police academy, which trains IPS (Indian Police Service) officers, teaches its candidates how to ride horses. It is believed that horse-riding helps one develop leadership skills.

Although horses are no longer used in warfare, they are a part of military history all around the world. Today they have more symbolic than real practical value in the armed forces. When the president of India attends any programme of national importance, he still enters in a chariot with a group of well-trained horses.

Next were the elephants. They have been the strength of our armies since times immemorial. Few countries can match India in terms of the quality and quantity of elephants. Chanakya had understood that the strength of our country lay in our elephants. In the *Arthashastra*, he talks about elephants in detail—capturing, training and caring for them, attending to their food requirements.

The king would be advised to take a daily supervisory round of the enclosure where they were kept. This shows how important elephants were for the king and his kingdom. Elephants were considered national assets of utmost importance.

It was a matter of celebration whenever a female elephant became pregnant. Much in the same way as we see a spirit of joyous celebration in our Indian culture when a girl is about to become a mother, provided with utmost respect, love and care. She is well-fed and tenderly cared for, and the family members give her extra consideration. Even the law of the land favours pregnant women. Most workspaces employing women offer maternity leave. Our culture and society provide nurturing facilities so that the girl can deliver her baby in an atmosphere of love.

Similar special treatment was showered upon pregnant elephants as they were invaluable assets to the state. There were special veterinary doctors and dieticians who would take care of them. The diet of a pregnant elephant was very different and highly customized—it took care of the nutritional needs of the animal. There would be daily check-ups by the physicians and reports would be generated every day.

Now let us look at war elephants. They were carefully selected from among the lot of elephants and then trained differently. They had special diets. In fact, it is believed that these elephants were even given meat and liquor. Can you imagine, elephants that are herbivorous by nature being given meat? It is important to remember that this was not meant for all elephants but for the special category of war elephants. War elephants had to be aggressive and prepared for attack. Liquor and meat in their diet helped foster aggression. Using his knowledge of Ayurveda, Chanakya also fashioned certain medicines for war elephants.

So the third component of chaturanga was the elephant, the power and might of the armed forces. Their sight itself was enough to make the enemy shiver. Armies that had no idea how to tackle elephants often suffered in such scenarios.

This was one of the methods used by Chanakya to defeat Alexander and his army. Imagine an opponent in war, who comes from a part of the world where elephants are not that common, being attacked by trained and powerful elephants. This can shake the confidence of the enemy's army. And Alexander's army did not know how to tackle such an attack. No wonder it was not easy for Alexander to think like Chanakya, for the latter knew the weakness of the enemy beforehand.

The final part of chaturanga comprised the soldiers. They were also called foot soldiers as they were last in the ranks. Yet, these were the soldiers who would be at the forefront of the battle. They would attack once they received the order. There is less strategic thinking involved in this group. They were men of action more than thought. If you look at chaturanga as a pyramid, the foot soldier made for the base of the pyramid, but it is important not to underestimate their importance.

For one, they came in large numbers. In war, numbers matter a lot; the size of the army matters. There are many strategic advantages one has when the foot soldiers are large in number.

Imagine a trained and well-equipped infantry. If you give them the best of weapons and the best of training, this last link of the army becomes its very strength. Another major factor that can make a difference is the weapons provided to the foot soldiers.

Kings played chaturanga to practise military strategy. Now let us look at the game.

Both players have the same numbers to begin with; they start on equal terms. The number of chariots, horses, elephants and soldiers are the same on both sides. Each player has to make calculated moves against his opponent. The starting point is the same. But the winner is always the one who makes the smarter moves.

It is all a game of permutation and combination. If one player moves, the other will also move accordingly. If one kills a soldier, the opponent will also kill one. The rules are the same for both sides. So, neither has any advantage over the other. It's the way a player thinks that makes the difference.

As battles are not fought on the battlefield but in the minds of the generals instead, chaturanga was often played to encourage strategic thinking and also to urge one to think of countermoves.

At times, one has to think ten moves ahead. Slowly, through the course of the game, as one is thinking of what the opponent may be thinking, one enters the mind of the enemy.

Chaturanga and the game of chess

Chaturanga is the foundation from which the modern-day game of chess has evolved.

Today, in the armed forces, playing chess is encouraged to build strategic thinking. It helps one develop the mind.

Of course, the game has evolved a lot since the time of Chanakya. Many changes have come about in the game of chess. But the game originated in India and is now played across the globe.

In its original format, chaturanga had only four elements in the army (chariots, horses, elephants and soldiers). Today, we find many additions to the game. The rules too have changed and evolved.

When it made its way from India to the Middle East, the first addition to the game was the camel. In India, except for a few states such as Rajasthan and Gujarat (Kutch region), where there are deserts, the camel is not very common. But in the Middle East, the camel, once introduced into the sport, became an integral part of it much like the horses and the elephants. Later, when the game found its way to European countries, many more changes were made, including the change in name to 'chess'.

Passing years have brought about further changes. The chess board is more defined now, with sixty-four squares, and more powerful pieces have been introduced.

Today, chess is an internationally recognized sport with competitions held around the world. It is ubiquitously stocked in all common places too, right from coffee houses to libraries.

That is how the game came to be what it currently is. But let us not forget that this game is of Indian origin and that Chanakya contributed to its development. He encouraged kings and military leaders to play it.

One cannot overstate the mental and intellectual benefits of this sport.

The rules of chess

Just as in the case of other sports, chess, too, comes with its own rules.

We must remember that chess is a war game, and so it adheres to rules just as is expected in a war. Chanakya often emphasized the need to follow rules scrupulously. Most times, these rules stemmed from fundamental values and principles. He often said that the spirit of the rules drives both the enjoyment and the winning factor of the game.

To understand how the rules were formed, one has to dive into the past and retrace them. They were mulled over for hours and deliberated over for years. There were endless discussions and debates, and through trial and error, they found acceptance.

However, these rules weren't chiselled in stone. They were subjected to varied criticism and circumstances before finally evolving into its present-day form. With such detailed deliberation and thinking, time continues to change the game. New rules are formed and the game continues to adapt itself to be accepted by the younger generations.

Swami Chinmayananda often said that every generation has two responsibilities—first, to continue with what is good from the past, and second, to change what is not required and is irrelevant now.

The passage of time has also seen wars change over generations. From horses, elephants and camels, today military forces have warships and nuclear weapons. But what has remained the same is the spirit of the rule, the principles.

Chanakya was a staunch proponent of dharma, which comprises ethics, principles and values. In the *Arthashastra*, which contains 6000 sutras on good leadership, he has used the word 'dharma' 150 times.

In the case of war, Chanakya talks about 'dharma yudh'—war with an ethical base, war fought not only for power, but also for truth. Therefore, in Indian culture, dharma is given a lot of importance. But this word has many facets. Dharma also means duty. For a soldier, it is his duty to fight the war.

Therefore, when we look at war from the standpoint of dharma, we see a different perspective. It takes into account both the winner and the one who is in the right. This is why the Mahabharata is also called a dharma yudh. It was not a war fought only to conquer Hastinapur. It was about who was on the side of the truth. In war, a side that is morally correct can defeat the largest of armies irrespective of its strengths or size.

Analysing chess from the perspective of dharma will offer keen insights.

The soldiers (pawns) are always the face

An interesting aspect of the game of chess is that soldiers always lead the group, neatly arranged in one line. This shows the respect given to them. The soldier is not as powerful as the king, yet he leads the army. Many times, we see leaders taking all the limelight, whereas in reality, it is the ordinary people who put in most of the effort.

A soldier in an army may not even have a say in matters of warfare. But in the game of chess, it is the other way round. He becomes the face of the army. He is given full credit and leads the army onto the battlefield.

The soldiers have their own power, even if it appears limited. They can only move one step at a time. Yet, this power is so important that, with it, they have been empowered to kill anyone. The small solider can use his power against any powerful person. He can even engineer a checkmate and defeat the enemy king.

The interesting thing is that if the solider manages to reach the other end of the chessboard, he can redeem one life for his army. Such a soldier can then be replaced with the highest power. Therefore, the most insignificant player in the team has the power to become its most powerful member.

Most importantly, the game always starts with the solider making the first move. Yes, when war is declared and the game of chess starts, it is not the king who moves first. It is the soldier who makes the move and the war begins.

The minister is more powerful than the king

This is another interesting aspect of the game. The king is not the most powerful person in the game. It is the minister. The king, like the soldier, can only take one step at a time. The only advantage the king has over the soldier is that he can move crossways on the board and can also retrace his steps.

The minister, also called the queen by some, is the most powerful. It is the minister who can crisscross throughout the board. Straight, diagonally across, one step or multiple steps, backwards, or forwards—she can do anything. This is the kind of power given to the minister in war as well. De facto, the minister is the commander and the real warrior of the game.

It is interesting to note here that the moves made by the queen on the chessboard, which is second in command, are used not only to attack but also to protect the king and other pieces.

Everyone has a different power

No piece in the game of chess is powerless. Each has been empowered with different moves. Depending on its designation and role, it has its own moves and steps. Not a single one sits idle, as all pieces, at any given time, play in sync with one another.

In most sports, there are extras. In the game of chess, though, there are none. All warriors are actively playing and everyone is involved.

While the knight, or horse, has a different kind of move (it moves two and a half steps at a time in an L formation), the rook, or castle, can only move straight, and the elephant can only move diagonally. All these different moves taken together make up the strength of a side.

Same rules for both players

There are two players in a game of chess, opposing each other, and each has an army on the chessboard. The same rules apply for both players. Even if one has been a winner in the past, the rules are not changed and they must start on a level playing field.

In life, too, everyone is given an equal opportunity. It is not that one is better than another. It is how we use these opportunities to our advantage that makes the difference. Which is why there is wisdom in always thinking carefully and then making our moves in life.

Checkmate

In chess, the king can never be killed.

This signifies how chess, as is the case in war, places importance on respecting each king. You need not kill the leader to defeat the enemy. Conquering does not necessarily mean killing. Even though the enemy is defeated, one should respect the leader.

There is competition in every sphere of life. But being part of the same profession, one need never disrespect the opponent. So what if he is out there to defeat us? We should win over the competition. But the captain of the other team should be given due respect right till the end. This is sportsmanship and reflects the spirit of the game, which is why it is called dharma yudh.

Alexander defeated Porus, who was then brought in front of the victorious king. Alexander asked Porus how he wished to be treated.

Porus, from the standpoint of an Indian value system, said that he should be treated in the same manner that one king should treat another. It took some time for Alexander to understand the context. But the rule in Indian war is that even a defeated king is to be treated as a king, with respect.

The game of chess, on the whole, allows one to see what Chanakya wanted to teach everyone.

7

The Ancient War Gurus—
Chanakya's Teachers

Om. Salutations to Sukra and Brahaspati

—Arthashastra, Opening prayer

Being a good student does not necessarily mean that one always has to stand first in class, be eloquent and academically brilliant. Yes, of course, all this can be an added advantage, but from the standpoint of the teacher, a good student is one who has the right attitude towards learning.

When we have the right attitude, we find that, over a period of time, even a seemingly struggling student understands the teachings better. Knowledge has subtle and finer aspects to it too. It is not just memory or retention that makes a student better. Rather, it is a deep insight into the subject that many are not able to grasp.

Good students may be ordinary, or even dull, in the beginning. They are, however, defined by their sincerity and dedication. They try to put forward their best efforts. They try to analyse different points of view. When the teacher notices the effort and humility of the student, she/he trains the student in a different way.

It is the old story of the hare and the tortoise. Patience and dedication make a successful formula. Sincere students are slow in the beginning, but they are steady. They keep moving and do not stop. On the other hand, the so-called bright students, who show greater confidence in the beginning, might fizzle out over time. It is not only the start that matters, but also the process leading up to the ending.

A good teacher is always a good student first.

Chanakya was one such example of a great student who transformed into one of the best teachers India has ever known. He learnt great lessons from teachers of war who lived before him.

Becoming the best student

It is important to adopt the attitude of being a good student first. This is vital to take one to the next level—of being the best. One need not aim to be the best; instead, one just needs to practise being a good student for a long time. The results come when the time is right.

When we look at the subject of war, where exactly do we find the connect with this aspect in the life of Chanakya? If we study and read about his life, we find a connection with war in the battle against Alexander, or when he dethroned Dhana Nanda. However, that happened at a much later stage, when he was applying his learnings.

The roots can be traced to the time he was a student at Takshashila, where he later went on to become a teacher. It was where that he was introduced to war theories and different models of war. In the gurukul of Takshashila, Chanakya learnt about the various teachers of war practices. That got him deeply interested in the field of military science and, slowly, he explored the subject in depth. Eventually, he became a master in that particular field. First, he mastered the theory, and then when the appropriate time came in life, he applied that knowledge on the battlefield.

Even today, the same rule applies in the life of any good military expert. When a person is recruited to the armed forces, he is trained. This training covers both aspects—theory and its practice. This is the starting point in the formation of a warrior. Good teachers or coaches help one obtain further insights into the subject.

Modern-day army officers, in their respective institutions, are first introduced to various theories. They are first good students of war science. Then they go to their respective fields and when the time comes, they apply these theories and become successful.

There is a voluminous amount of literature available in the field of military strategy and military science. There are many journals, films, videos and courses available on the subject. There is no dearth of material for anyone looking to dive further into the art of war.

The various war gurus mentioned by Chanakya

One of the best things about the ancient Indian education system is that the process of acquiring knowledge never started with just one person. So it is difficult to trace the original teacher of a particular subject. There was a continuous flow of knowledge, and every generation added to the field with its own research, thinking and contribution.

There is a process in our ancient system called 'shastrata', meaning debate and discussions on the shastras, or scriptures. A group of scholars would get together and discuss various dimensions and aspects of a subject. They would talk about their experiences and opinions. They would also quote from the various scriptures they had studied. These mature discussions are very much a part of the entire canon of Indian literature.

These discussions would continue for days, weeks, months and years, sometimes even spanning across generations. These discussions were aimed not at finding what was right and wrong, but exploring and discovering newer dimensions to the subject.

In earlier times, there was a lot of mutual respect among scholars. Each scholar was a champion in her/his chosen field. When a scholar made a statement, it made sense. When another one counter-argued, it was with reason. These discussions would continue while the young students watched these experts debate. In our Indian scriptures, there is a philosophical method called 'nyaya', logic. Chanakya used this base of logic and called it 'aanvikshiki'.

While writing the *Arthashastra*, this methodology (tantra yukti) was used for debate and discussion (*vada* and *samvada*). Chanakya would bring in various points of view of previous teachers of arthashastra to discuss the art of war.

The process of discussion comprises what is called 'purva paksha' and 'uttara paksha', meaning the opinions of yesteryear (purva) scholars and those he considered present-day scholars (uttara). One may not agree with the former teachers, but one should definitely listen to their opinions and discuss them in detail before giving one's own point of view. At the same time, a senior teacher respected a young champion disproving his point as well.

We see the respect given by Chanakya to the previous war gurus from the opening statement of the *Arthashastra*. He starts with a prayer or dedication to the most well-known teachers of the science and art of war.

'Om. Namah Sukra Brahaspatibhyam'
(Om. Salutations to the great teachers—Sukra and Brahaspati)

These were stalwarts in the art and teachings of war. Sukra, also called Sukracharya, was the guru of the demons, or rakshasas. Brahaspati, on the other hand, was the guru of the gods, or devas.

There is a clear contradiction here. In our Puranas (ancient Indian literature that are a part of our rich spectrum of scriptural mythology), we find numerous stories of king and saints. We also find stories of gods and demons fighting against each other. Now, in a battle among the gods and demons, each had their own gurus. These gurus were wise people and experts in the field of war. So the demons were guided by Sukracharya, while the gods were guided by Brahaspati.

These two great teachers were also strategists in battle. Naturally, since their own students were fighting each other, the gurus would want their respective students to win. Therefore, it would actually be a battle of the minds of the teachers.

If you are a student of the art of war, whom will you study, the guru of the gods or the guru of demons? Interestingly, the demons lost most of the times and the gods were always the winners in the long run. So, it would seem better to study the winning guru, Brahaspati, right?

This was not so for Chanakya. He would first salute the guru of the demons and then the guru of the gods, first paying his respects to the losing side, then the winning one.

There is a Sanskrit shloka which says: 'Durjana pratama vandanam, sajjana tadanantaram.'

It translates to mean that one should salute the durjana (the wicked person) first and then the sajjana (the good person). In short, salute and give respect to both. There are a few implications and lessons here for students of the art of war.

4. We must never build any opinion about anyone from the beginning. Be open-minded. A person

who goes into the battlefield with a fixed mindset and opinion will not have options available. An open-minded person is flexible and ready to learn. We need to learn from the best and the worst, but have the attitude of a learner.

5. There is something good in the bad person, and there are some flaws in the good too. Before we form an opinion of who is good or bad, or right or wrong—for we should surely take a side—we should listen to both sides. In the court of law, the judge never gives a judgment without listening to both sides. The court of law is meant for debate and discussion.

6. In the same way, one needs to look at all factors in war and think them through. One has to be ready to listen to all sides before making a judgement of who is right and wrong. However, after all due consideration, the final judgement should be made in the mind.

7. The wicked are often ahead of the good. They think differently and are ahead of their times. They spend a lot of time calculating. They are constantly thinking of various options and strategies. So, if you get inside the mind of the wicked, it's really interesting to see so many possibilities. Chanakya, being a good student of the art of war, did not miss any opportunity to

see another viewpoint, which the 'right' people may have missed.

There are at least fourteen other arthashastras mentioned in the *Arthashastra* of Kautilya. The treatise refers to many earlier authorities and their opinions on war strategies. There are, in all, 112 places in the text where such opinions are articulated.

There were schools which taught arthashastra and the art of war. There are, in all, five schools of thought that Chanakya discusses in his *Arthashastra*.

1. The Barhaspatyas
2. The Ausanasas
3. The Manavas
4. The Parasaras
5. The Ambhiyas

The Barhaspatyas are mentioned in six places, the Ausanasas in seven, the Manavas in five, the Parasaras six times and the Ambhiyas once.

There are six individual teachers mentioned and their opinions ascribed in twenty-eight places by Chanakya in his *Arthashastra*.

1. Bharadvaja (seven times)
2. Visalaksa (six times)

3. Pisuna (five times)
4. Kaunapadanta (four times)
5. Vatavyadhi (five times)
6. Bahudantiputra (once)

And then there are cases where the names of the teachers are not mentioned, but they are referred to in general terms as 'acharya'. There are fifty-nine cases where opinions are attributed to the teachers, a term referring to most of these predecessors. Twice, we see mention of words such as 'eke', meaning 'some' or 'one', and 'apare', meaning 'others'.

For a student interested in knowing each of these war gurus, a detailed study of the *Arthashastra* is suggested. One of the best commentaries on the *Arthashastra* is by R.P. Kangle. He was a Sanskrit professor at the University of Mumbai and he also translated the book into English. The book is available in Sanskrit and English. One can easily buy the book—*Kautilya's Arthashastra: A Study* by R.P. Kangle—in any bookstore that sells books on Indology. (Indology is the subject of study and research on Indian wisdom. It is a very well-respected branch of study across the globe dealing with other subjects as well, including yoga, Ayurveda and so on.)

Apart from R.P. Kangle, there are other scholars too who have worked on translations of and commentaries on the *Arthashastra*. Shamasastry (who discovered the original manuscript of the *Arthashastra* written by Chanakya in 1904 in Oriental Research Institute, Mysore University) is one of them.

The intention is to draw attention to these scholars who have done an in-depth study of the *Arthashastra* and kept the work of Chanakya alive and available as a rich resource for future generations.

Mahabharata and the art of war

In order to understand India, one needs to study the Mahabharata. It is supposed to be the largest epic ever written in the history of mankind. It has one lakh shlokas, and they cover every subject in this world.

The Mahabharata was written by Ved Vyas, an intellectual. He was a man of destiny, born to fulfil a deeper purpose. His profound achievements made him a legend. Ved Vyas lived almost 5000 years ago, as a great scholar, a recognized saint, a missionary and a guru to all gurus. His life continues to inspire people even today. Many may not know it, but one of the most important days in the Indian calendar is marked 'Guru Poornima'. This is the day on which all gurus in the Indian tradition are remembered. This day is actually the birthday of Ved Vyas.

Ved Vyas's work in the field of literature is vast and holds tremendous value. He compiled the four Vedas (Rig Ved, Sama Ved, Yajur Ved and Atharva Ved), wrote the eighteen Puranas (Vishnu Purana, Garud Purana, Shiv Purana and so on) and the Bhagawat Maha Purana. He also wrote commentaries on the Upanishads and the Brahmasutras.

However, the jewel in the crown of all his work is the Mahabharata, a monumental work and a magnum opus by all standards. It is said that it is so comprehensive that one need not read any other book. There's a saying, 'That what is not there in the Mahabharata is not there in Bharata.'

It covers the widest range of events that Indian mythological history encompasses—including the eighteen-day war, and all the incidents that mark the lives of the Pandavas and the Kauravas. The epic dives into the strategies used on the battlefield, and even the weapons and methods used to inspire legendary warriors such as Arjuna.

All of the acharyas of warfare that Chanakya mentions in his own *Arthashastra* come from the Mahabharata. There is a clear connection between the two texts. However, the Mahabharata has the larger canvas.

Expansive as it is, the epic gives keen insight into the intricacies of war. Knowledge of military warfare is not be complete without the study of the Mahabharata. Let me give you a personal example.

I have been teaching at the National Defence College (NDC) of India. This is the best government institution in India as far as the study of military science is concerned. The best of officers from the different armed forces attend the courses conducted here. It is situated in New Delhi, and the participants are intelligent and well-experienced. The average age group is over fifty-five years old, and they have led wars and experienced and mastered a lot more.

Interestingly, I was among the youngest teachers at NDC. But my humble knowledge of arthashastra has given me opportunities to teach the 'best' Indian war wisdom to the 'best' defence officers of our nation.

Once, during my lecture on Chanakya, I mentioned the study of the Mahabharata and its war strategies. There were nearly a hundred students in that batch and many of them were pursuing their PhDs in military study.

Later, I had forgotten that I'd mentioned the Mahabharata, as my subject was arthashastra and Chanakya. At the end of the course, I was called to meet the participants before they left, along with the lecturers who taught the batch. Very soon, they were to get promoted and lead larger teams and shoulder bigger responsibilities in the army, navy, air force and the paramilitary forces.

At that time, a senior participant came to me and said, 'Sir, I am thankful for your introduction of the Mahabharata during the course. After you left the campus, I started to study the epic. I have travelled across the globe and studied and met some of the best scholars in the field of military science. But, when I started reading the Mahabharata, everything seemed insignificant in front of it. There is so much that the Mahabharata has to offer us in the field of warfare and now I feel sad that I was unaware of it for so long.'

I felt a sense of pride to have introduced the text to this senior officer.

The senior official went on. 'In the few remaining years of my service, I will make sure that the study of the Mahabharata is reintroduced in our Indian armed forces. I promise to continue studying and teaching it for the rest of my life.'

This is the power of the Mahabharata.

Some prominent war teachers

Here are some of the revered teachers who taught warfare to their students:

Bharadvaja

The foremost among the teachers is Bharadvaja. The commentators of the *Arthashastra* usually identify him as Drona. Dronacharya, as he is well known in the Mahabharata, was a teacher to the Kauravas and the Pandavas. When the cousins—the Kauravas, a hundred of them, and the Pandavas, five of them—were young, they attended the same school. This was the elite school where children from the royal families studied.

But Dronacharya is respected and counted among the best teachers in archery and mantra shakti. In Chapter 12.138 of the Mahabharata, there is a discourse on politics delivered to King Satrumtapa by Bharadvaja, also known as Kanika.

Kanika Niti is another book which has its roots in the Mahabharata. It is still used as a treatise on political wisdom and as a reference manual on warfare strategies.

Visalaksa

'Visalaksa' means 'the broad-eyed one' and it is, according to the Mahabharata tradition, the name of Lord Sankara himself.

It is believed that Lord Shiva was the original guru of all gurus, and therefore he was also called 'Adi guru' or first guru. He was the teacher of Danda niti, or political science, and had bestowed upon mankind complete knowledge of the science of politics and the art of war.

The sheer quantum of knowledge was very vast, but given the limitations of human life, one could not learn everything in one lifespan. So Lord Shiva condensed the knowledge to fit into 10,000 sections. This was later shortened by Indra, the king of gods, to 5000 sections, which was subsequently further shortened by others to 1000 sections. Kautilya, or Chanakya, uses this wisdom from Visalaksa and further reduces the number of sections in his own *Arthashastra*.

Bahudantiputra

Bahudantiputra is supposed to be the name of Lord Indra. The name apparently signifies 'the son of one whose arms are the teeth'. In fact, the Mahabharata mentions the Bahudantaka Shastra, implying that Indra himself was known as Bahudanta, or, 'having many teeth'.

Indra is not just an individual god; the name also signifies a position—it is the post reserved for the leader of the gods. But no one person can sit on the throne forever. So, when one king retires, another takes over. But one of the major responsibilities of a king (Indra) is to pass on the knowledge of the science of politics to the next generation. Therefore, in India, we followed a tradition where kings used to document their wisdom and experiences. Apart from the philosophy of how to run a kingdom, they would also mention the systems and processes of good governance. This was later used by succeeding kings, who themselves would pass on their experiences and wisdom.

Pisuna

Pisuna, according to the commentators, is the sage Narada. This reference came about perhaps because the name signifies 'a tale-bearer'.

Narad Muni, as he is popularly referred to in the Puranas, was a scholar of great repute. He was an excellent teacher. He would tell stories and, through his songs, pass on wisdom to kings. The best thing about Narad was that he was accepted by all the kings, be it the ones on earth (bhoomi), the heaven (swarg), or kingdoms below the earth (patal).

He is also known to be mischievous. He would initiate wars among various kings. But the intention behind these acts of mischief was not merely to instigate fights, but also to teach moral values. He is known as the ambassador or envoy of Lord Vishnu, one who would execute the steps necessary to address challenges facing governance.

Kaunapadanta

Kaunapadanta, the commentators say, is to be identified with Bhishma. In the Shantiparva of the Mahabharata, Bhishma is made to appear as a teacher of the shastras.

Bhishma, a venerated hero in the Mahabharata, is again considered to be among the greatest warriors of all time. Though he fought on behalf of the Kauravas, he knew that the Pandavas were essentially on the right side of dharma. But he was bound by his commitment to the oath he had taken to protect Hastinapur.

The advice given by Bhishma to the Pandavas at the end of the war is immortal. It forms the basis of raj niti wisdom. There is an exhaustive mention of war in this section of the Mahabharata. Furthermore, in this part of the epic, Bhishma also advises on the subject of respect for women in a society.

Vatavyadhi

Vatavyadhi, whom the commentators identify as Uddhava, was the minister of Sri Krishna.

A childhood friend of Krishna, Uddhava was a teacher himself. He was a scholar in the bhakti (devotion) tradition. However, he was also an expert in warfare. He is known to have taught and practised the same along with Lord Krishna.

Krishna, as an able king and administrator of Dwaraka, had Uddhava as his minister. The way Uddhava held the administrative post of an able minister was later taught as a lesson to students. His administrative insights were also used by Chanakya to govern the Maurya dynasty.

Others

There are many teachers whose names have been mentioned by Chanakya. The list is exhaustive, and some of the names are not clear indicators of the person or the teacher they refer to. It appears that some of the names of these teachers are nicknames ascribed to them based on some physical or mental peculiarity associated with them.

Lastly, there are numerous cases in which the opinions of the acharya are stated and, in most cases, refuted by Kautilya, who then adds his own opinions.

'Acharya' is a generic term for any teacher. So it can be an individual or a school of thought. But all of them have been given their due respect and credit by Chanakya.

The process of study

The art of war and the study of military science, as with any other field of knowledge, keep expanding and growing over time.

There is a process behind the study involved in this field. The men we study in this field are experts who not only make assertions but also back them up with study and research.

Let us look at the process Chanakya followed and taught:

1. Define the field

Clarity of knowledge on the topic one is looking to study is vital. Lack of clarity can lead to confusion and wastage of time. The topic here is the art of war. So, when the subject is clear to all students, it allows them to be focused.

After one is clear about the field of study, one has to try and gather maximum information about that field. It is at the helm of the copious material available that one can start the journey of acquiring knowledge.

Chanakya was very clear that his field was political science and economics, or arthashastra. This includes the art of war as well. It was with full awareness of this that he started gathering information.

2. Forming one's own opinions after studying other experts

Scholars or experts in a field contribute to the existing body of knowledge. Studying them gives perspective and allows one to see other dimensions on the subject. At times, contradictory views and opinions can get confusing. But it is important not to get burdened by them. We need to have the basic fundamentals in mind in order to carry on and form one's own opinions.

Chanakya did study the various acharyas and built on their past wisdom. However, as a thinker, he had his own independent views and opinions. That is why Chanakya is considered an original thinker and his version of arthashastra is considered an original work.

3. Respect others

In the field of knowledge, there are people who try to establish themselves, but in the process, do not give credit to others. This is not good for any expert, researcher or scholar. We need to respect others in the field of knowledge. Only then will we be able to develop humility, which is the basis for wisdom. A wise person is humble, and humility brings wisdom. 'Vidya dadati vinayam'—meaning, knowledge gives humility to a person seeking it.

We find this evident in the opening prayer of the *Arthashastra* that we saw earlier—'Om. Namah Sukra Brahaspatibhyam'. Chanakya mentions and gives respect to all his previous teachers. Imagine taking the wisdom of others and not giving them credit. That would be intellectual theft. And therefore, today, the law protects a person's ideas legally through Intellectual Property Rights (IPR). Chanakya, though, did not live in a generation where IPR was a legal responsibility.

8

Becoming a World Conqueror ('Vijigishu')

This science (of Arthashastra) has been composed for
the acquisition and protection of this world and of
the next.

—*Arthashastra* (15.1.71)

It is a myth that India was never a world conqueror.

Yes, surely, we were and still are a peace-loving
nation. It is not that we were lazy and did not have
dynamism. In the past, we have by and large maintained
a winning spirit.

Everyone respects such a country. In the present era,
we find this kind of strength shown by the United States
of America. Not only are they economically superior,

but they also aim at being world winners in science and technology, art and culture, sport and innovation, education and research; they want to retain their 'numero uno' position everywhere.

This sense of superiority in the thought process comes from a certain kind of attitude and mindset. Usually, it starts with the leaders and then, slowly, it percolates down to every common man. Soon, it becomes the very spirit of the nation. It is difficult to change such an attitude when it perpetuates over time and generations together wield their subtle dominance over others.

The British colonial rule is an example. They went about conquering the world. They lived up to the saying, 'The sun never sets on the British empire.' They held sway over a territory so large that their influence spread to almost every part of the globe.

Before the British, it was the Spaniards who enjoyed such world dominance. And prior to that, the Portuguese. History provides brilliant stories of such mighty empires. It is quite fascinating to learn about these world leaders who conquered vast territories during their golden period.

So, in a way, we see that conquering and ruling over the world is a common desire exhibited by most powerful kings. Such an attitude is encouraged in most cultures of the world. To grow is a natural phenomenon. When it comes to leaders who head kingdoms and countries, such an attitude is a sign of success and might. However, the method used in holding such power should not be harmful to others. Only then is such a world conqueror both respected and loved.

In India, too, from times immemorial, we have evinced ambitions of conquering the world. From the days of the Vedic period, the age of the Puranas, and even in the age spanning the events recorded in the Mahabharata and the Ramayana, there are many mentions of world conquerors.

In the Mahabharata, there is a mention of the 'Ashwamedha yagna'. It is a ritual from Vedic times used by ancient Indian kings to prove their sovereignty. A horse accompanied by a king's warriors is left to wander for a period of one year. In the territory traversed by the horse, any rival can dispute the authority of the king by challenging the warriors accompanying it. After one year, if no one has managed to kill or capture the horse, the animal is guided back to the king's capital. Then the king is declared an undisputed sovereign.

There were many such rulers in Bharatvarsha. The Vijayanagara Empire had spread its territory across the borders of their kingdom. Shivaji, who led the Maratha Empire, had conquered and established his might in many parts. The name 'Chhatrapati' conferred on Shivaji means 'a great king having a large empire'.

We have had a rich legacy of leaders in India who expanded their kingdoms far and wide. They were not just destroyers, but also known to be rulers of high repute and ethics. Some were even considered noble kings with a spiritual outlook. 'Shrimanth yogi' was a title conferred on Shivaji; the term means 'a yogi who is rich and prosperous'. This was because he had established dharma in his kingdom and the vast empire under his reign.

Chanakya would call them 'raja rishis', a term that refers to a king who is a saint, a seer and an able administrator, before whom enemies would bow down with reverence.

In foreign policy, the goal set before a ruler is that of expansion. The ruler should be 'vijigishu', that is, 'desirous of conquering' other territories. Therefore, to aim to be a conqueror is a good attitude to have. However, it is not just about being one who slays enemies. A killer instinct without actually killing is what is really required. This kind of a world leader requires having an attitude with a different philosophical dimension.

Hence, Chanakya, in his *Arthashastra*, had classified the conqueror into three types. Each of these has a different attitude and strategy to conquering the world.

The three types of conquerors

1. **Dharma vijayin**—one who makes conquests for the sake of glory and is satisfied with the mere submission of other kings.

2. **Lobha vijayin**—one who makes conquests out of greed and is out to obtain land or money or both.

3. **Asura vijayin**—one who makes conquests in the manner of a demon and seizes land, money and the wives of the conquered king, and takes the opponent's life.

This classification of conquerors is mentioned by Chanakya in his *Arthashastra*, Book 12, Chapter 1, sutras 1-16 (12.1.10-16)

Let us examine them here in detail.

1. Dharma vijayin (the righteous conqueror)

The word 'dharma' has been explored in detail in the *Arthashastra*. As we have seen, it means righteousness, a moral and ethical way of doing things. So, a conqueror who uses the right method, in the right, ethical manner, is called a dharma vijayin.

The righteous conqueror is satisfied with submission. As we have seen in the case of the Ashwamedha yagna, the horse is sent to various places. The kings of those respective kingdoms will accept the authority of the king who has sent the horse and will submit to his leadership. It is important to understand that submission here is not surrender. The king will still continue to rule his own kingdom, but he will accept the overall leadership of the other king.

Let us understand this with a modern-day political example. In India's current political system, there are various leaders appointed at various levels. In a democratic system, people are voted to power. India, as a nation, is a union of many states put together. So, the chief minister of a particular state remains a leader in the state, whereas the prime minister is accepted as the overall leader at the national level.

The power of the chief minister is not diminished in any manner by accepting the overall authority of the prime minister at the central level. At the state level, one continues to be a leader of that particular state. This is a type of submission, or acceptance.

Yet, a chief minister of any state can aim to become the prime minister. He needs to follow due process. If a chief minister is voted to power and accepted as prime minister, he becomes the national leader. The other chief ministers then have to accept his authority. It is important to note that this position of overall authority is often temporary, and as history has shown, new leaders will emerge from time to time.

Similarly, if one desires to be a vijigishu, a world conqueror, the process is to be followed in a democratic way, where others can accept or submit to the authority. In such a process, there is no bloodshed or killing of people. There is an acceptance of power by the others in an ethical manner. This category of rule is called dharma vijayin, or the righteous way to become a world leader.

There is one more side to this kind of conqueror. He has to take on the full responsibility of protecting the smaller kings who submit to him. The vijigishu may have a larger army, and the submitting kings may have a smaller one. However, if anyone attacks the smaller kings, the vijigishu should make sure he protects the king who has submitted to him. His army will be sent to protect the other kingdom, or the armies of the vijigishu and the smaller king will merge to become one powerful army in the event of an attack or danger from others.

Once again, taking the example of India as a nation, most of the states have their own police force to deal with criminals and those who create internal rifts. However, the national army intervenes when things get out of control. When an external enemy attacks the nation, it is not considered an attack on a particular state in a particular region. It is an attack on the country as a whole. The Indian armed forces would have to step in to defend this particular area that has been attacked. Thus, faced with an external aggressor, the whole nation and its defence forces merge into one total unit. In that unity, they win as a team.

Oftentimes, smaller kingdoms who see danger looming are advised to submit to the vijigishu as the larger army would protect them. The vijigishu, being a dharma vijayin, will accept the task of protecting this smaller kingdom. Thereby, he will also be able to expand his territory. A dharma vijayin is not an opportunist as we may assume. In this case, it sees the smaller kingdom's protection as its dharma, for it is strong and it is its duty to protect the weak.

This is not too dissimilar from the family as a unit. Within families, we might find that the younger brother does not like accepting the superiority of the elder. But in the eventuality that the younger brother is attacked by an external enemy, in order to protect the house and family, the elder brother has to intervene. In such circumstances, if the younger brother comes to seek help and submit to the elder, it is the duty of the latter to use all his resources to protect the former. And once the external enemy is gone, the maturity and the leadership of the elder brother are naturally proved.

Leadership is apparent when one protects the weak because it is a matter of duty and not a display of power.

A dharma vijayin has a very similar attitude. He is not driven by power. Rather, he is driven by duty. Once the duty is fulfilled, he easily foregoes the power that he has.

Power for a dharma vijayin is temporary; rather it's a responsibility.

This feeling of responsibility over power is what makes a great leader. When the time comes to give up power, the dharma vijayin will do so without any attachment.

> A feeling of detachment and a spiritual bent of mind are essential in becoming a dharma vijayin.

In the Ramayana, we find that Rama had the opportunity to take over as the king of Lanka after killing Ravana. He could have become the supreme authority in the newly conquered kingdom. In fact, who would not have liked Rama leading Lanka? Even the citizens of Lanka would not have denied it as Rama was the conqueror. However, instead of taking over the throne of Lanka, Rama handed over the same to Vibhishan, the younger brother of Ravana.

We also need to note that Rama was the king of Ayodhya, which is a comparatively smaller kingdom than Lanka. Also, it is believed that Lanka was made of gold. It was said to be much more advanced in technology; it had made great progress in aviation, as seen by the Pushpak Vimaan. Had Rama taken over Lanka, he could have expanded and ruled a much larger kingdom than Ayodhya.

Yet, Rama was a dharma-bound leader. He knew his objective was not to conquer the kingdom of Lanka, but to bring back his wife, Sita. Also, Rama felt that Vibhishan was more deserving of the position of ruler as he understood the kingdom better.

When Rama was handed the leadership and the throne of Ayodhya too, he was guided by his sense of dharma. This is why he decided not to take the crown as Kaikeyi had demanded the crowning of her son Bharata as king. No one would have denied Rama the throne, and in fact, he was the ideal and efficient leader by all parameters. Yet, he felt it was morally incorrect to take over when the queen had demanded that her son become the king.

So by giving up the kingdom of Ayodhya and also the chance to rule Lanka, what did Rama actually gain? He conquered the hearts of one and all, he won the love and respect of the citizens of both kingdoms. This is a true case of a dharma vijayin—asserting moral superiority over positional superiority.

Interestingly, both Bharata, ruler of Ayodhya in Rama's absence, and Vibhishan, king of Lanka, accepted Rama as their de facto king. They submitted to his leadership. They, in fact, became his devotees.

Such kind of leadership is very rare in other parts of the world. What makes the dharma vijayin mode different is this very behaviour and the ability to not get carried away by power. This is India's contribution to concepts of world leadership. This kind of philosophical approach makes our thought leadership quite unique and different.

2. *Lobha vijayin (the greedy conqueror)*

The lobha vijayin, or greedy conqueror, is only satisfied with the seizure of land and goods. He is out to reap economic benefits. He is greedy and unsatisfied. To acquire more is his primary motive.

Such people are not wealth creators; they covet others' wealth. They constantly have an eye on others' lands. Instead of looking at what he already has, the lobhi (greedy) person will look at what others have and is happy when he fills his coffers with what rightfully belongs to others.

His treasury, even when full, does not satisfy him. There is no limit to his quest for conquest. To conquer the whole world and its wealth is his only objective. He will expand his territory until the last village in this world is under his command. He experiences a sense of superiority over others through the very size of his kingdom. To exacerbate the situation, such a conqueror not only targets big kingdoms but also small, helpless ones, all for the sole purpose of making his own treasuries overflow.

Chanakya specifically points out two methods that a lobha vijayin uses to expand his kingdom and loot others. These two methods are land and goods.

Land

Land is a limited resource. Only one-third of our planet is land, and human population grows rapidly by the second. With land, one builds cities, tall buildings, dams, bridges, temples and monuments to showcase one's power. But this becomes difficult when the land available starts becoming limited.

This limitation is sought to be overcome by 'growing vertically'—erecting buildings that are taller and taller. Financial capitals such as Mumbai, New York, London, among others, now have innumerable skyscrapers. In the case of smaller, yet economically strong countries, such as Singapore, the demand for land leads to a rise in its price.

So what is the solution to the problem of limited landmass when it comes to a king or in the present context those desirous of acquiring land? Acquiring land belonging to others is the answer. This is the reason why real estate has become a defining factor for any economy across the globe.

The stories of voyages, from Columbus, who discovered America, to Hudson, the explorer who found Canada and parts of north-eastern United States, show how the acquisition of land was valued. Alexander too wanted to conquer the world. In short, he wanted to expand his physical geography, and acquiring the territories of others was the method many like him chose.

Goods

A greedy person, when in a foreign area, has his eye on all that he does not possess. Similarly, a lobha vijayin, doesn't only look out for jewellery and other ornaments, but also for other forms of physical wealth.

The crops, the various idols and ornaments in temples, the antiques of a place, even fruits, vegetables, spices, and other precious materials are looted. The merchants acquire the same via trade, while a lobha vijayin does it via wars.

There are some questions that arise here. For example, what is a small, ethical, self-sufficient and happy kingdom to do if a lobha vijayin attacks it and tries to loot the land and wealth?

Chanakya gives us a solution to deal with such a lobha vijayin. He advises taking the help of a mitra (an ally) with whom the armies can be combined. In case this is not a viable option, yield money to the attacker. Yes, the correct way to tackle a greedy person is through money. The important thing to note here is that one should not part with land. This is because land is an asset that should not be given away at any cost. Once land is lost, one cannot get it back easily. Money given away, however, can always be generated again.

> Give money and goods to the aggressor and satisfy him. Then slowly plan strategically and defeat the enemy through other methods.
>
> —Chanakya on how to defeat a lobha vijayin

There are many countries that were attacked and its residents forced to flee their lands. They had to struggle for generations to build their wealth in the new places where they lived as refugees. The land they lost will perhaps never be theirs again.

So it is important to understand the value of land as an asset over physical goods. When we study the various wars that have taken place in varied cultures around the globe, we find that one of the prime objectives was to conquer more land. Generations may have changed, but human beings still consider land to be one of the most important assets they can possess.

3. *Asura vijayin (the demonic conqueror)*

The third type of conqueror is called an asura vijayin. As the name suggests, it is the asura, or demonic, method of winning over. They have no rules in war.

This demonic conqueror is satisfied only when he has taken everything available—land, goods, sons, wives and lives. This is what sets him apart from the lobha vijayin, who is satisfied with money and land.

The asura vijayin feels that no method is wrong if it helps achieving total power. He will take the children, rape the women, kill every last man and burn down cities. The demonic presence in him reigns in its full glory.

These are the tyrants, the dictators, the autocrats. Such conquerors are cruel and oppressive in nature. They are cunning and crooked. One just cannot trust them. What they are thinking is a mystery to everyone. Even their own men, ministers, soldiers and family members, are not spared if they feel their power is threatened.

Their only objective is absolute power. A father will kill his son for power. The son too won't hesitate before killing his father if he is asura-like in nature. Brothers and sisters are not spared either; even teachers and spiritual gurus are murdered if they come to lecture them on moral standards. Asura vijayins create havoc wherever they go.

No emotion guides them bar one. They understand only one language—that of absolute power. Moreover, such conquerors do not appreciate logic or systematic discussion. Many times, such rulers are nice people and seem to be good leaders. But, if they ever feel threatened that their power will be taken away from them, they turn into violent beings.

In the life of Krishna, we find his uncle, Kamsa, was of such nature. He was a good person who loved his sister. He held a lavish wedding for her. But the moment he was told that the son of his sister will kill him one day, he changed completely and showed his true colours.

He got his sister, whom he dearly loved, along with her husband, imprisoned. He kept a careful watch over them. The moment his sister gave birth to a child, he would kill it. Seven children were killed the moment they took birth.

This kind of violent streak is precisely what makes them asuras by nature. These conquerors are demons in human form. They go to any extent to destroy anyone who seems harmful to them. Some even go to the extent of killing others just for fun.

In Puranic stories taken from Indian literature, we find many such asuras. They go to forests and trouble hermits. They destroy ashrams. If priests are conducting any rituals, yagna or homa, they vandalize the whole place. There is no reason why they do this. They just feel that it is fun to indulge in such cruel activities.

The harassed priests run to gods or the kings to seek help. Oftentimes, we find gods and kings coming to their rescue. Benevolent kings and their armies would hunt down such asuras and kill them.

Does Chanakya have any advice on how to deal with them? Is there any way to win them over?

The strategy given is:

'By yielding land and goods to him, he should take counter steps, remaining out of reach himself.'

—*Arthashastra*, 12.1.16

First of all, to appease such conquerors, one must give them something. To begin with, one must not retaliate. Instead, one must distract them by yielding land and goods to them.

Unlike in the case of a lobha vijayin, where the idea is to not give land but only goods, here Chanakya recommends giving both land and goods. It is important to run in this case. It is not too dissimilar from an instance where we are holding an object that has caught fire. We should let go of it and save ourselves.

We need to protect ourselves first. If we live to fight another day, we can always return to retrieve what we have lost. What good is land and goods that we possess if we are not alive? It is important to prioritize life over goods and land.

The moment the asuras get the land and goods, they find temporary satisfaction and their minds are diverted to something new that they have just conquered.

And once we are far away and safe, we must think of steps to be taken against such tyrants. It is difficult to think straight during a crisis. One needs a peaceful state of mind to plan and have a counter strategy. So the rule here is to buy time from the opponent.

Later, we can brainstorm with others, or approach a friendly kingdom and seek an ally. Whatever be the case, we must never accept defeat. This is Chanakya's winning strategy.

And when the time comes, with the right methods, weapons and moves, we win back our kingdom using full force against the demonic conqueror. In life, winning should be an attitude.

But when it comes to winning over others, one must use the dharma vijayin method and become the conqueror of not just lands and kingdoms, but the hearts of everyone.

This is the concept of vijigishu—a world conqueror.

9

Different Types of Powers to Become a Winner

He should establish contacts with forest chieftains, frontier-chiefs and chief officials in the cities and the countryside.

Arthashastra (1.16.7)

'I am powerful.'

Being arrogant can turn power from being the greatest strength to becoming the biggest weakness.

'The enemy is also powerful.'

This second statement keeps us grounded. We must never take our opponents for granted even if they seem small and weak. The enemy may have an advantage which we may not.

It is important to have our head firmly on our shoulders while fighting a war. As we have seen in previous chapters, war can be destructive and can throw the whole society out of gear. If war is absolutely unavoidable, its consequences need to be borne in mind beforehand. Only after carefully considering all aspects of war should a leader march against his enemy.

While teaching his students at the gurukul one day, Chanakya asked them what strategy is.

After receiving many answers, Chanakya put forth the answer in a simple and effective manner. He defined strategy as 'considering an action along with its consequences'.

In other words, every action has a reaction. If one can judge the possible reaction to a particular action, one can plan accordingly and not be caught unawares. What happens when one throws a stone in a pond? The stone hitting the water creates ripples in the water in the form of circles. And these circles, much like waves, spread out. One who understands that ripples are a natural consequence of a stone hitting the surface of the water is not taken aback. In fact, one will enjoy the sight of those ripples expanding from the centre, and will happily throw more stones into the water, taking delight in the act.

The acharya explained the importance of understanding the nature of actions and their reactions.

If one does this, one will not be taken aback and can enjoy the interplay of action and consequence in any situation in life. He told the students that a true warrior is never caught off guard on the battlefield. He knows every action and reaction beforehand. For any move made by the enemy, the warrior does not even raise an eyebrow. And this is the difference between an ordinary warrior and an excellent one.

A student commented that this almost sounded like knowing the future, as if everything could be predicted.

The guru agreed. He added that once one is aware of an action and its consequences, the future is indeed almost known. Even so, one should not take things for granted. One can never tell how things might turn out. Perhaps, while you are studying the enemy, the latter is in turn studying you. Thus, one must always stay alert and vigilant because the enemy, too, wants to predict the future and turn it to his advantage.

Another student posed an interesting question: how could one acquire expertise in strategy and know about actions and their consequences?

Chanakya replied that there were methods in which strategies are developed. He mentioned writing about it in detail in the *Arthashastra* and gave a few tips.

He started by talking about having a strategic mindset through swadhyaya, vriddha-sanyogah and aanvikshiki. He then went on to explain these methods.

Swadhyaya means to study. If one studies recorded strategies and written documents from the past, one will be able to learn and understand what others did in similar situations. So the wisdom and experience of the teachers of war strategy can be used. These stalwarts had sound ideas on how to prepare for war, and what to do after the war was over. When one studies such examples, one gathers know-how from the experiences of others and this helps build strategic thinking. Then with the help of others' ideas, one can develop one's own ideas as well.

This is what good warriors do. Apart from building their own strategies, they study other warriors and their methods. Good warriors are keen observers and learn from other experts.

When we study, our mind opens up to various possibilities. We do not repeat the mistakes committed in the past. From past strategies come strategies beneficial for the future.

Vriddha-sanyogah entails learning by meeting experts in warfare. This is better than studying about them. Living legends in the field of warfare are experienced and have seen wars at close quarters. There is a much bigger advantage in meeting an expert face-to-face as compared to studying written documents. One can actually discuss details, ask questions and clear one's doubts. What one cannot do sitting with books, one can do in the presence of an expert.

Aanvikshiki is the science of thinking. This is a subject close to Chanakya's heart. When one can think properly, one will be able to develop better strategies. Thinking is difficult. One needs to develop a habit of strategic thinking. Even swadhyaya and vriddha-sanyogah are incomplete without aanvikshiki.

When the students couldn't properly grasp the meaning of aanvikshiki, the acharya explained the logic of 'thinking through' all the gathered information and experiences of experts. He discussed the process of thinking deeply so as to distil and assimilate all the information within us.

It is not enough to simply gather information, get a new idea, a different point or dimension provided by others. It needs to be mulled over, looked at critically. It is equally important to think about the practical application of the idea.

Chanakya further simplified it by giving the analogy of a cow.

Have you noticed how the cow eats grass during the day and chews the cud later at leisure? It will keep chewing till it assimilates every aspect of the grass. The cow does not simply swallow the grass but makes sure the grass is digested properly by its prolonged chewing.

This is how one should be thinking. One should take a point and think over it again and again till one gleans new dimensions from the wisdom of others.

Different types of powers

What makes a person powerful? And what is the power that makes a person really successful?

Chanakya did not consider the power of the position, chair or designation as the ultimate power. One may be the king or the leader of a country or a community. Yet, there is always the danger of being dethroned. Only when a person understands what real power is will he remain undefeated forever.

Chanakya has himself explained these powers that lead to final success in war and everything one undertakes.

He says: 'Success is three-fold: That attainable by the power of counsel is success by counsel, that attainable by the power of might is success by might, that attainable by the power of energy is success by energy.'—*Arthashastra* (6.2.34)

In Sanskrit, these powers are—mantra shakti, prabhu shakti and utsaha shakti.

Let us look at each of them in detail here.

1. Power of counsel (mantra shakti)

Mantri (minister) comes from the root word 'mantra', which also means advice. Thus, the real duty of a good minister in a kingdom is to give sound and wise advice that translates into the real power of the king.

Therefore, Chanakya suggests that a leader should always be surrounded by people who are better than him. These ministers will give him sound and unselfish advice. A person evolves through people who give him inputs. Company makes man in the truest sense.

There is a famous saying that goes, 'You are an average of five people whom you surround yourself with.' It means that the people who surround us will influence us and our thinking. If we think about it, right from childhood, it is our loved ones and friends, our surroundings that have most closely influenced us in becoming who we are today. The moment we change our surroundings and inner circle, our thinking also changes. And we become totally different.

The kind of people and advisors one needs has to be carefully considered. Chanakya says that a king's mantris have to be carefully chosen. Because therein lies the real power of the king—in the power of the advice that he gets.

It has been proven that ordinary people who got good advice rose up the ladder to become successful. While those who were brilliant often lost the way in the absence of right advice. Therefore, it is also important in situations of war that one gets the right strategic advice. One who listens and implements the advice of experts emerges a winner.

We have seen in the earlier chapters how the advice Krishna gave to Arjuna made the biggest difference between winning and losing the war. While the Kauravas had a larger army than the Pandavas, the latter emerged victorious as they followed the right and timely advice of wise persons. On the other hand, the Kauravas also had good advisors in the form of Bhishma and Vidura. Not following the advice of these wise men cost them the war. Shakuni, their prime advisor, had a selfish, ulterior motive that resulted in the Kauravas being unable to distinguish between right and wrong.

Anyone on the battlefield should have the basic intelligence to differentiate between good and bad advice, should be able to tell the difference between right and wrong advice. Only then will they be able to take advantage of the advice given. One also needs to develop the quality of humility in order to keep learning from others.

We should not make anyone and everyone we come across our advisors. There are qualities to be tested in the person we turn to for advice, so that we are sure that what we are receiving is sound advice. In the *Arthashastra*, Chanakya gives many tips and suggestions on the method of choosing the right advisors.

What are the qualities of a good advisor?

There are many according to Chanakya, but a really good advisor is one whose advice helps you win and succeed. Ultimately, results matter. Once we have the desired results in place, we know that the advisor was valuable. What is the use of an advisor when none of his advice works?

Good advice not being carried out properly is the fault of the person receiving it. Yet, no advice is good if it does not yield results. Therefore, the first and foremost quality of a good advisor is that he must give advice that is not just conceptual or theoretical, but practical and actionable.

Say, in the case of war, if one is advised to have the best of weapons to fight the enemy. This seems like good advice, but suppose the reality is that one cannot afford to buy the best weapons, what should one do? The advisor cannot simply say, 'Go and buy the best weapons.' This may not be practical. So, what is the next best advice? Can one make use of existing weapons? Or is there a better method to win the war beyond employing the best weapons?

The next important quality of a good advisor is his experience in the field. The best advice comes from those who have themselves used it. They know if it works or not. For example, if a person had defeated the enemy in a past battle, he can speak from his own valid, rich experience.

The present war may be totally different from the past experience of the advisor. Yet, his experience counts. He can bring in a new dimension in the current situation; he may be able to give a practical suggestion to apply to the current scenario.

Another important quality of a good advisor is that he should not be selfish in the advice he is giving. Often, there can be a hidden agenda in the advice being given to a person in power. The advisor may be looking for some benefit, such as power, money, etc. Such a person cannot be trusted. In reality, that is not advice at all. It is a selfish agenda in the guise of seemingly helpful advice. The advisor has to be totally selfless in doing his duty. Such advisors are rare indeed and are to be sought in times of need.

Yet another valuable quality of an advisor is that he should not insist on his advice being carried out. Even though he is clear while giving the advice, he will not force its implementation. There is a kind of detachment required while giving advice. Many times, the biggest problem does not have anything to do with getting right advice, but its implementation with the receiver.

In the Mahabharata, we find that Duryodhan had many good advisors, including Bhishma, Dronacharya and Vidura. Even Krishna had advised him to share the property with the Pandavas to avoid war. Advisors have to accept the situation as it is, whether their advice is being followed or not. They have to accept with grace the possibility of their advice not being accepted.

And even if the other person accepts the advice and follows it, the advisor should act as a catalyst that is part of the process, yet is not involved in it. He does not take the credit for anything that happens. Even in case of success, a good advisor should say, 'It is all because of the person who did it.'

All in all, the best advisor is one who gives sound advice with a lot of maturity, experience and wisdom. But it has to be coupled with detachment and a sense of aloofness. He needs to be able to look at the problem from a distance and at the same time be close to it.

This is the power of advice. When a king has such a wonderful team of advisors, he is truly powerful. And such power ensures victory in any battle.

Chanakya was asked by one of his students whether one can have multiple advisors.

He replied in the affirmative and added that that it is always better to have more than one advisor. The number of advisors should be just right, not too many nor too few. If one has too many advisors, one may get confused. But if one has only one advisor, one will have access to only one perspective and only one dimension of thinking.

So, an ideal number of advisors to have is three to four. They will bring in different viewpoints to bear on the subject at hand. It is essential that one gets new dimensions and alternative ways of thinking about any subject one is dealing with.

Chanakya also warned his students that it is not just the number of advisors that matters, but also the maturity, experience and wisdom that they bring in while giving the advice. The acharya indicated that the quantity as well as the quality of the advisors matter.

Thus, having a good number of advisors of top quality is what brings more power to the king. If a leader wants to have more power, the advisors should be equally good.

When it comes to mantra shakti, Chanakya wanted his students to be lifelong learners. In the art of war, things keep changing from time to time. War is a game of minds, it is a game of thrones and a game of thorns. Moreover, it is definitely a game of power.

And to become a winner in war, the ultimate power game, let us have the best of intellect on our side, because in the end, war is not just a military affair but also an intellectual battle. Thus, one should have the best of intellectual warriors on one's side to be sure to win the war.

2. Power of might (prabhu shakti)

The mighty are powerful. The powerful are mighty.

Chanakya talks about one of the most important powers—the power of might. It is called prabhu shakti. This kind of power comprises a display of external might, which includes the treasury and the army.

Economic and military power combined together is called prabhu shakti. Even if we have one of these we are considered powerful. So one can only imagine the power one attains when both economic and military powers come together. Any enemy would think a thousand times before waging a war against such a powerful entity.

Let us look at economic power and military power individually.

Economic power is something the world understands easily. There are many types of wars, as we have seen. One of them is trade wars that are based on the power of money. Nations that are strong economically, who control the international economy, control the world. They have a major say at world conferences.

'Artha eva pradhanah'—wealth alone is supreme, says Kautilya. Chanakya, who makes this profound statement, is well known as an economist who understood that there is something about the power of wealth to which people easily surrender. *When the power of wealth arrives, all other powers lose their significance.* Control over the treasury is synonymous to control over the whole kingdom.

Therefore, in wars, one of the main objectives is to attack the treasury first. Once the treasury is looted, this gives the power of wealth to the enemy. However, if the treasury is safe, the war is far from over.

Of course, today we do not have large physical treasures as in the olden days, when kingdoms held gold, gems and jewellery. These have now been replaced by banking systems that are characterized by numbers and digits along with currency notes and other formats of modern transactions. Yet, there is a continuous threat to the treasury. The objective now is to protect banks from threats, such as cyberattacks, hacking, and so on. Which is why software security measures, such as firewalls and other kinds of technological shields, are built around the treasury.

A growing economy is important in guaranteeing the success of a nation. The bigger the economy, the more powerful the nation is. While writing the *Arthashastra*, Chanakya spoke of many measures to enhance treasury tax collection, and other systems were introduced to generate revenue to be added to the treasury.

Even smaller kingdoms and countries can be powerful by using economics as their biggest weapon. It is not just the size of the kingdom that matters, but also its financial condition. We see many countries that have a large mass of land, but geographically large countries may not always be powerful. A small country such as Singapore, on the other hand, is considered powerful thanks to its prudent economic policies. In a considerably short period of time, Singapore moved from being a Third World country to a First World nation.

Another reason for this progress is the quality of leadership that Singapore has. Lee Kuan Yew, who is considered to be the founder of modern Singapore, has worked hard for decades to make the country economically stronger. The leadership in Singapore gave primacy to economic power. Chanakya had suggested the same centuries ago. A good leader has to focus on economic strength that gives might to the nation. Singapore has an army that is small in size, yet its economic strength provides an advantage that offsets its size.

Military power comprises the army, navy, air force and paramilitary forces. The weapons that a country possesses, its soldiers along with excellent generals as its commanders and its leaders make up its military power which boosts the might of the nation.

Not only are a strong army and good generals required, but the strategy used is equally important. There exist think-tanks and advisors to the army too. These bring intellectual strength to the army that determines how the army performs.

Another strength of the military is information gathering. There are intelligence systems imbibed in the military. They keep collecting news about all that's happening on an ongoing basis. Gossip and discussion in the enemy camp are closely followed. From time to time, this information is used against the enemy.

Another important aspect of military power are the weapons. If the enemy possess a weapon, we should have a better one than that. If we do not possess good weaponry, the enemy can easily overthrow us. This is why we find that, today, to show military strength, we need to have nuclear weapons too in our arsenal.

In the olden days, warriors performed penance to obtain divine weapons from the gods. And these divya shastra, or divine weapons, provided them competitive advantage over the enemy. In the Mahabharata and the Ramayana, we find various warriors performing penance to amass divine weapons which were then used against the enemies.

'Prabhu' means leader. It also means god, or 'ishwar'. To develop this kind of power is essential. A person with economic and military strength cannot be defeated easily and by retaining this kind of power within his control, such a person will continue to be in power forever. There is hardly any power in the world that can overthrow the power of might.

One may wonder whether it is possible to have power if one does not possess money and military forces. What about someone who wants to be in power but has no economic advantage. Has one lost the game even before one begins?

There is a third type of power that matters the most. Even if one has nothing, one can emerge victorious. How does one do that? How can one having nothing create everything? The third type of power comes to our rescue. It is called 'utsaha shakti', or the power of energy.

Once a student asked his guru, 'What can one man alone do?' The guru laughed and said, 'In fact, it is only one man who can do.'

He explained further, 'The person who is all alone can take the first step and initiate the process. Then the rest will follow. A leader who takes initiative will soon start gathering followers. And these followers will then become an army. And these committed followers also create economic strength.'

With a smile, the guru added, 'So what if you do not have any other power? You are the power of all powers. You seek the power within you. You have the potential to become the most powerful. Invoke the leader within you . . .'

Let us delve deeper into the power of energy.

3. Power of energy (utsaha shakti)

There are many meanings to the Sanskrit word 'utsaha'—zeal, zest, enthusiasm, spirit, vigour and so on. One of the most important translations of the word in English is 'energy'.

For our convenience and understanding, we will refer to 'utsaha' as energy. Utsaha shakti can thus be translated as the power of energy. It cannot be understood simply as the power of any person. It is better understood as the energy of a leader.

If the king is energetic, the subjects will also be energetic. If he is slack and lazy, his subjects will also be lazy, says Chanakya. Therefore, the energy of the leader is the energy of the team as well. The speed of the leader is the speed of the team.

'Uth' is the root of the word 'utsaha' in Sanskrit. It means to 'get up'. It implies taking oneself to a higher level. So, with energy, one can rise and climb higher. The current situation may be very bad. It may not be encouraging and it may not be to our advantage. Yet, if one decides to get up and take charge, things can start improving.

If a person just sits downcast and does nothing, there is no scope for improvement. The situation will only get worse. Once a person decides to act, there is hope. Hope should be translated into action. A good action plan will lead to success.

Chanakya states that only when a leader decides to do something about a situation does it improve.

We must not sit and brood over our problems. Problems will never get resolved by themselves. That is just wishful thinking. Problems require people to solve them. Only when a person engages with a problem will the problem start suggesting solutions to us. If we do not act, the problem will only worsen with time.

Remember the adage, 'A stitch in time saves nine.' It is true in the case of problems. The moment we see a problem, we need to nip it in the bud itself. Let us not just sit and wonder, otherwise the problem will become bigger and bigger.

When Alexander came to India, all the other kings kept sitting quietly. It is not that they did not know of his mission to conquer the world. They were aware of his arrival and that he had already defeated Porus. Yet, they did not understand the gravity of the problem. Many of them did not look at it as a problem at all. In fact, they considered it someone else's problem.

Chanakya recognized the problem and came up with an action plan against Alexander. He had the energy to get up and address the problem head-on. If Chanakya had not taken the first step, the country would have been annexed by Alexander. The energy and enthusiasm of Chanakya saved the nation.

Another interesting dimension of utsaha shakti is that it can be transferred to others too. Enthusiasm is contagious. An energetic person can inspire others as well. Inspiration leads to inspiration. It is like a chain reaction. One energetic person drives the next, and within no time, the whole place can become a powerhouse.

An inspiring leader motivates many in his team. He propels them onward in his mission. When the mission is coupled with a vision, transformation happens. In no time the whole vision and its energy are translated into concrete results.

In the case of war as well, what if the enemy is stronger and mightier than us?

We may not have the best of weapons. We may not have money. But we have 'us', we have our own selves to draw upon. When 'we' start, everything else starts. Energy has a snowballing effect. When a snowball rolls, it only becomes bigger and bigger. It takes up such a mighty form that the opponent is overwhelmed into either surrendering or being defeated by the energetic opponent.

This is how great leaders fought. They had the power of enthusiasm, the power of energy, on their side. Which led them onward not only to winning wars but also to achieving the progress of a nation.

Let us now summarize the three types of powers that Chanakya defined for us. These are mantra shakti, prabhu shakti and utsaha shakti. Even if we have one of them, we can become successful.

However, possessing all three will ensure that no opponent in the world can defeat us. The very presence of these three powers will shake the enemy's morale and they will stand defeated even before the war begins. So let us all build on these three types of power to become eternally powerful and remain indefatigable.

With the advice of great men, we should build our war strategies. With economic power, we should become wealthy. With the might of military power, we should have a strong army equipped with the best of weapons. And finally, we should have the power of enthusiasm and energy with us.

Swami Chinmayananda, the great spiritual master, said: 'Enthusiasm is the fuel required in any project you undertake. That will finally lead to success.'

10

Tips to Win Our Daily Battles

One question at the core of all that I write is: *Is the wisdom of Chanakya relevant to my readers?*

I strive to make sure that I do not simply glorify the great teacher. Yes, he was a great man who lived nearly 2400 years ago, but his teachings resonate even today.

He was a philosopher and teacher in the true sense of the terms. But Indian philosophy has an advantage—it is time-tested and will be tested every time. In every generation, people will debate and discuss whether a philosophy is still relevant and gives the same benefit that it provided generations ago.

Nevertheless, history has shown that Indian thinkers and philosophers did not like to rest on their laurels, glorifying the past. They wanted to debate and discuss. Argue, agree and disagree, if required. From these discussions would emerge something new and relevant to that particular generation. That is how knowledge expands, grows and finds its relevance. That is how wisdom becomes time-tested.

The same principles are applicable to the experience and wisdom of Chanakya.

While discussing this particular text with my publishers, Penguin Random House India, I asked my editor, Milee Ashwarya, 'How do we make *Chanakya and the Art of War* relevant to our generation?'

We then came up with the idea of including a final chapter containing tips on how to win our daily life battles. The editorial team was very happy with this practically valuable, additional chapter in the book.

The text until now has focused on the art of war as seen in the *Arthashastra*. But then, the reality of the present-day generation is different. We are a very lucky generation; hardly any of us have actually witnessed wars in the real sense.

There were two great wars in the twentieth century—the world wars. From these emerged the United Nations, which strives, through worldwide representation, to contribute to the development of the human race. But wars of that scale have not been fought ever again in recent times, which is why I call it good times for the human race.

I have many friends in the armed forces who joined the army, navy or air force with a spirit of 'do or die'. But they are all now retiring from their jobs without having fought in a single battle or war. They have no first-hand war stories to tell.

On the other hand, these times of peace have also seen the highest number of suicides. It is quite strange indeed. While millions used to die in wars, today millions die due to 'inner enemies'.

These numbers are growing every year across the globe. From children and teenagers to mature adults, people are giving up so easily on the challenges of life. How can this generation, which has the benefit of technology, communication, access to information and easy travel, value life so little?

That's when we wonder if the enemy has been internalized? It appears that we are not equipped to handle stress. We cannot deal with the simple problems of life. We are a lonely generation. We have probably solved and understood how to avoid external wars, but what about the inner wars and conflicts we go through on a daily basis?

Who will teach us how to kill the inner enemy, the negative mind, the mind that gets stuck in a situation and does not find any solution? And the easy escape route seems to be to end one's life. Suicide is not a solution to problems. Chanakya did not appreciate people who committed suicide. In the *Arthashastra*, there is a mention of punishing those who committed suicide by not allowing them funerals, as suicide means that a person has given up on the challenges that life has thrown at him.

In Indian culture, it is believed that one who commits suicide is only delaying life's problems as these problems will reappear in the next life. So why not face the challenges in this lifetime itself?

And that is exactly where Chanakya helps us. While he has taught us the art of war for an external enemy, we can use the same principles to defeat the inner enemy— our weak mind.

Rhetoric such as 'be positive', 'think positive', only help to a certain extent, providing only temporary relief for the pain experienced by a person. Most of the time, rhetoric offers only surface-level medication.

Therefore, it is imperative to look at some practical solutions that work. I am confident that these methods will work for all, just as they have worked for my former students.

These ten tips given by Chanakya can be used anytime and anywhere. They can be used individually, or in combinations. We must bear in mind that they may seem superficial at first, but constant practice will bear fruits. If one can make one's mind strong and strategic in nature, one can win any battle in the world.

1. Never fight a battle alone; take along a friend (mitra)

Life is full of battles and it often seems like a struggle. From the moment we wake up until the time we go to bed, there are myriad problems that we come across. If we do not know how to handle situations when we are awake, nights can become sleepless too.

Stress is a primary problem plaguing this generation. Stress to some extent is natural, but if we do not handle it, it can become a problem that consumes us. Today, mental health is one of the biggest challenges facing us. If not handled in the right manner, it can lead to depression and bring on suicidal tendencies.

> Chanakya's solution for stress is as simple as talking to a friend.

When we have a friend with whom we can share and express our problems, it makes a significant difference. As human beings, we require fellow beings to share our feelings with, to discuss and debate and ultimately feel good. Technology cannot replace human interaction. It is important to understand the importance of having a group of friends who will be with us through thick and thin.

The same advice is given by Chanakya while building a kingdom. In the Saptanga model of a kingdom, one of the most important pillars is 'mitra'. Even the king requires a mitra, or a friend, to run his kingdom effectively. Imagine the kind of stress that a leader of a kingdom faces. She or he would have to bear full responsibility for keeping all the people of the land happy. Administration is a stressful activity. Yet, how does the leader keep cool and calm in the midst of all these challenges?

If the king is not able to find a solution to a problem, he can go to another friendly king and discuss the problem. It is possible that a solution will emerge following the discussion.

Friends act as more than mere listeners. They are people whom one can lean on and get advice from.

2. Listen to the wise (vriddha-sanyogah)

Senior citizens are an extremely neglected lot in society today. Traditionally, India has had a joint family culture, which includes the elderly in the family. Nowadays, people are moving away from this and resorting to nuclear families. This has led to a lot of stress in working couples and single parents.

It is generally believed that senior citizens are liabilities to a family. Children are growing impatient as they have to take care of the elderly, and when parents are sick and have outlived their utility, they become liabilities. Rising medical and living costs aren't helping either.

Can these so-called liabilities become solutions to our current problems? Chanakya says, yes, they can. Senior citizens are assets to every generation. We should know how to give back to them for all they have done for us.

In the daily battles of life, these senior citizens can be very helpful. One may wonder how. The biggest advantage of senior citizens is that they have time and experience to offer. The younger generation has neither of the two. So, in reality, the two could fit together like a perfect jigsaw puzzle. It can be synergetic.

Let us consider a practical example that I recently came across. There was an orphanage where children longed for the love of parents. Right across the road was a home for the aged, neglected parents of well-off children. The children wished they had the love of parents and grandparents. And the senior citizens longed to have their children and grandchildren with them. A brilliant social worker came up with the idea of merging the orphanage with the home for the elderly.

Imagine the transformation that took place. Senior citizens were surrounded by children, who were active and vibrant. They found joy once again in their lives. And the children were fed and taken care of by the elders, who became their parents and grandparents.

This concept embodies vriddha-sanyogah— association with elders. They take care of us much beyond our expectations. Elders have nothing to expect from life. The next generation, on the other hand, has a long life ahead. But, when the elderly come forward to guide the next generation, they create a win-win situation.

It is important not to neglect senior citizens in one's house and family. Our generation needs them as much as the elderly need the youngsters. There will always be some difference of opinion between generations. This is natural. However, love is what keeps a human society going. With love we can fight the biggest battles of life. A person without a family has already lost half the battle. Members of a family make sure that each one is taken care of and emerges as a winner.

3. When dealing with the powerful, keep in touch with a higher power

There is always a frustration when we have to deal with a difficult boss. Those who have gone through it know what I am talking about. If not, let's try and imagine the situation of a person who works day in and day out, for years, in the same office. And at the end of the hard work he puts in, all he gets is a message of dissatisfaction from his boss.

There are countless people who face this in workplaces all over the world. They work eight to ten hours every day under such pressure for a senior who never seems satisfied with the work done. Even their best effort goes unrecognized. Every day is a battle. A battle that will last as long as the employee retains the job, or the boss remains in his seat of superiority.

So what is the solution? The easy way out is to resign and find another job. Is there an alternative, though? The softer way is to accept it as a part of life and continue working. Listen to the senior's opinion from one ear and let it go out from the other, as they say. At least, the employee is drawing a salary and there is monetary happiness at the end of the month.

But there is a solution that Chanakya offers as well. That is, to think through the situation and find out what makes the boss a boss after all. Is it not that she or he is more powerful than the employee in designation and salary? The boss has more decision-making power than the employee. Now, what we need to remember is to learn how to crack the power of the boss.

We must realize that even the boss has a boss. So, if we understand the higher power, we can deal with the lower seat of power easily—this actually gives us a strategic advantage.

Chanakya says, 'While dealing with a strong king, take a stronger king on your side.' Automatically, due to fear of the higher power, the person we are dealing with comes under our control. Some people take the route of the court of law. When we have legal power on our side, our strength increases. So, if we have a superior harassing us, we must never lose confidence. We must take some advice and hit back hard. Let us think of the #MeToo movement that gained such momentum in recent times. The victims gave it back. Of course, some people misused it to settle petty, personal scores. But overall, most women benefited by giving it back to their bosses and other oppressors, using the might of social media.

I have a friend who had worked in a company for fifteen years. When a new boss came in, he started troubling my friend. Frustrated, my friend asked me, 'How do I deal with him? After all, he is the director of our company. Do you have a Chanakya strategy I could use?'

I smiled at him and asked, 'Who is higher than this boss of yours who is the director?'

His reply was quick. 'The chairman of the company to whom my boss reports.'

I suggested, 'Your boss is powerful. But do you have access to the highest power—the chairman?'

He thought for a while and said, 'Yes, I have been working in this company for a long time and the chairman knows me personally.'

Before I could speak further, he said, 'But this immediate boss of mine will not allow me to go to the chairman. And even if I do, he will come to know of it and he will give me more mental agony.'

I thought for a while before suggesting, 'Ok. So let's access the highest power indirectly then. Is there any advisor whom your chairman listens to, whom you know?'

His eyes lit up. 'Yes, of course. Our chief accountant. He is a school friend of mine and we stay in the same colony . . .'

'There lies the solution,' I said and smiled. 'Talk to your friend and communicate the same to the chairman.'

Relieved, he put the idea into action. Thus, my friend solved the problem.

Let us remember never to be afraid of power. There is always a higher power that we can access. If not directly, we can try the indirect route to success.

4. War is a mind game

Henry Ford once said, 'If you think you can, or if you think you cannot—either way you are right.' Chanakya would also give similar advice.

Most of us do not lose the war on the battlefield, but a lot earlier. War is always a mind game and, therefore, Chanakya would prepare the minds of the warriors first before sending them to war. It has been proven by research that winners in all fields actually visualized it even before they attained victory. Be it the sportspersons who won Olympic gold medals, or business tycoons who became billionaires, or those who became presidents or prime ministers of nations. All of them motivated themselves first.

Therefore, it is essential that in your mind you are clear about winning. The rest will follow. Where the mind is not conditioned or blocked by the negatives of failures, one will get fresh ideas required to fight the daily battles of life.

A common example comes to mind. Whenever there is a public transport strike in Mumbai where I live, when trains, buses or taxis do not ply, many commuters avoid going to offices. They feel it is not possible to go since their regular transportation is on strike. They do not think of any alternatives.

Interestingly, it is precisely that day it is easiest to reach office, a lot earlier than the usual time. In case cabs are not working, the government decides to put extra buses on the road. The roads are empty, and this sight evokes fear, so many people do not come out of their houses. The smarter people, though, see a strategic advantage here. They set out of their houses and take the first available ride and reach office faster. Usually, such a day is the most productive day too, as fewer people turn up and one can focus on one's key priorities and be effective at the workplace.

Once we take the first step towards our goal, the rest is easy. After all, we have reached the goal inside our mind. The rest is just a matter of time.

5. Advisors can make you or break you

In daily life, we have to be mentally alert. We must be aware that we are receiving various thoughts and opinions from different people. Apart from human beings, we are constantly being bombarded with information from the Internet, social media, radio, newspapers, television, books and other mediums.

Such information overload becomes dangerous after a point. We get thoroughly confused with contradictory views on a particular matter. To take a simple everyday instance, while some say that ghee, which is a traditional component of Indian cuisine, is good for health, others say it's saturated fat. What does one do in such situations?

First things first. Gathering too much information is not good. We need to be selective in what we read and watch. We get into discussions that really do not matter to us. How does it matter if X sportsperson gets married to Y cinema star? It's ok to add our bit to some social updates happening around. But it is not worth thinking too much about such matters.

A happy person keeps her/his mind free of stupid and irrelevant thoughts. We must choose our ideas and thoughts carefully, consciously. The same applies to the choice of our friends. We need to be discriminating in selecting the books we read. Most importantly, we must choose our advisors carefully.

Advisors can make or break us. If we get stupid advice, it can ruin our whole life and career. In the most important moments of our life, where decisions are critical, it is vital to have good advisors on our side. When we have to choose a career path, or join a new educational programme, let us ask for the right guidance from the right teacher and not just from our friends who may be equally confused.

The most important decision a person makes in her/his life is marriage. It involves choosing the person with whom we will be spending the rest of our life. Here, too, sound advice, in the form of a good matchmaker, marriage counsellor and family support, is required.

Chanakya suggests we choose our advisors with care. They should be mature and wise. They should have the necessary experience and they must also look at our well-being as the top priority. He also suggests that one should not have just one advisor, but about two or three of them. Not too few, not too many. When we take expert advice in any matter from three good sources, we gain access to better choices while taking a decision.

We must make a list of experts in every field, persons who will guide us in our career, education, married life, financial dealings and everything that is important to us. Such people will help us win the battles of life. Such wise people also help us avoid the pitfalls that we may come across. They are the safety net we have provided for ourselves.

6. Lift your people to the next level

This is the advice given to people in power. We saw an example of how to deal with people who are more powerful than us. But what if we are the one in power and hold an authoritative position?

There is a problem in being powerful. Either we can look higher to see who are more powerful than us, and seek to aim higher, or we can look below and see how many people are looking up to us, since we are in the position of authority.

A true leader is not one who wants to scale the ladder of authority. A true leader, according to Chanakya, is one who takes care of his people. Such a person, who looks at the welfare of his subordinates, automatically, by default, rises higher up the ladder of leadership.

So, if we are blessed with a certain level of leadership and authority, let us lift our people to the next level. Let us not keep the people below us confined to only the lower levels. We can train them, educate them, give them some bigger responsibilities, and looking at their capacity and capabilities, even promote them.

A true leader is one who creates more leaders. In daily life, let us remember we are fighting a battle. But the reality is that on a daily basis, we are also preparing for the bigger battle of the future. So when the war finally arrives, our team should be ready to fight for us. They should take up the challenges and come along with us. If we do not train our people and equip them with better skills, weapons and education, how will they face the bigger wars?

So, let's lift our people. Build their morale. Give them some freedom. Empower them with more trust. And slowly, each of the team members will shine to give their best. That is how, slowly, on a regular basis, we can build our team. Spend time with them. Guide them. Talk and discuss matters with them. Attend to their problems immediately. If we care and show it, they will reciprocate.

Shivaji, who built the huge Maratha Empire within one generation, knew of this strategy of Chanakya. His ministers were empowered and they fought the battles for their leader. When they won the battles, the ministers were put in charge of the newly conquered territories. The ministers then became kings in those respective regions. If Shivaji did not have a team of good and trusted ministers, how would he have expanded his base?

One single person is not enough. A team is required. And the team should be trained by the leader itself.

We must think about it every day. Are we a true leader? Are we supporting, helping and empowering our juniors? Chanakya has written about this in detail in the *Arthashastra*.

7. Study every day (swadhyaya)

One faces problems every day. From the moment one gets up in the morning to the moment one goes to sleep at night, one has something or the other to do. Daily life involves many unplanned and routine activities.

At times, we feel everything is fine, while at other times, we feel life slipping away.

Chanakya recommends a technique to keep the mind in control. He suggests that the best way to handle everyday problems is to study every day.

Chanakya is suggesting not just academic study. He is indicating something higher, also called swadhyaya. This includes worldly as well as spiritual study. The highest form of study is the study of scriptures.

When we read them regularly on a daily basis, we acquire a direction for our lives. We develop moral values and we also get inspiration from the wisdom of great people before us. A daily study of the scriptures is akin to consuming a daily capsule of nutrients. While nutritious foods and supplements give us energy for the body, the scriptures give us energy for our mind and intellect. They give us direction and help us solve the challenges we have to face.

Gandhiji used to say, 'When disappointment stares me in the face and all alone I see not one ray of light, I go back to the Bhagavadgita. I find a verse here and a verse there, and I immediately begin to smile in the midst of overwhelming tragedies—and my life has been full of external tragedies—and if they have left no visible or indelible scar on me, I owe it all to the teaching of Bhagavadgita.'

This is the power of swadhyaya, the study of scriptures on a daily basis. Every country, religion, tradition has some books of wisdom. Studying them regularly helps gather the right momentum for the required direction. Like an unknown power, it comes to our rescue during the most difficult situations we face in life. It gives us a road map when all paths seem stuck.

Chanakya made sure that in the daily timetable followed by a king, there were at least a few hours dedicated to swadhyaya.

8. Know the strength and weakness of the opponent

Some people are born smart, some acquire smartness along the way, some others remain ordinary, and the rest die as fools.

Having a strategic mindset is an important skill one should be able to develop.

A smart person is one who is able to accurately judge others. He is constantly studying and analysing, trying to understand what is going on in the mind of the person in front of him.

There are various methods Chanakya has suggested in the training of a leader. One of them is 'deh vidya', or what we call 'body language' today. The body has its own language. Most of us know about verbal communication—what a person says. But there is non-verbal communication as well. If we can study the body language of a person, we can understand what is going on in the mind of the person.

The same goes for the methods used by Chanakya in his war strategies. He is continuously studying the opponent. The enemy is being scanned minutely by Chanakya.

Can this technique be used in our daily lives? Yes, of course. We can observe people around us—when we take a walk in any public place, be it a garden, railway station or bus stand, the marketplace or when we are at a café or bar where people hang out.

Let us look at the way people move about and that can tell us a lot about what they are thinking. If we practise this, we will be able to develop the art of observation.

9. Honour scholars and thinkers

There is a basic problem we face in our generation. Teachers are a part of our lives only during the days when we formally study in schools, colleges and universities. However, this was not the case in the previous generations. Students were connected with their teachers, lifelong. Tutors were a part of their lives on a regular basis.

One major advantage this had over today was that the students had a perpetual guide by their side during any trouble they came across in life. These gurus, teachers and acharyas knew their students personally and guided them accordingly. It was like having a family physician. This doctor was not just a physician; he was a friend, philosopher and guide.

The teacher knew the student's problem well before time. He also knew what would work for his student. At times, the problem was not at a physical level; it was psychological. So he would suggest treatment accordingly. Each solution was tailor-made for the individual, as what may work for one may not work for another.

The teacher, at times, simply lent an ear. This simple act can sometimes make all the difference. A patient hearing is all that a person requires at times. This is no ordinary family doctor; obviously, he's more of a strategist.

We must take time to think whether we have access to a teacher of this kind in our life. This is someone who has been a lifelong mentor, a friend, philosopher and guide in every stage we have crossed. Those who already have one are lucky. For the others, it is important to look for such a mentor. Then no mountain or obstacle in life will be insurmountable. Such mentors will be our daily inspiration.

One of the best ways to start looking for such a master is by respecting scholars and thinkers.

Chanakya himself was a scholar and a thinker. Because he was respected by the students, he made them kings and emperors. We can all see the transformation he brought about with Chandragupta Maurya. From an ordinary student, Chandragupta was moulded into one of the greatest leaders in the land.

Chanakya also trained his students to respect other scholars and thinkers. If a scholar ever wanted to meet the king, it became a priority. The king even offered his throne for teachers to sit upon. In return, their guidance helped him rule the kingdom more effectively.

It is easy to seek the company of scholars, teachers and thinkers. Readers can easily find them at schools, colleges or universities they have attended. It is important to keep their company lifelong. Let us help them a bit by doing some service, and they will guide us multiple times.

Once we have a thinker on our side, battles can be won easily. Once we have a teacher on our side, she or he will be our strategist in the daily battles of life.

10. Teach children to be materially and spiritually successful

Expecting our children to be successful is a natural feeling for any parent. But what kind of success do we want children to pursue? Unfortunately, the definition of success has changed.

Success has become limited to children doing well in career and financially. There is no doubt that being materially successful is important as far as worldly achievements are concerned. But are we neglecting another important aspect of success—the spiritual side?

There is a story in the Upanishads. Swetaketu, a brilliant boy, came back home after his studies from the gurukul. He had been away for twelve years. And when he reached home, his father, a great rishi himself, asked, 'Do you know everything? Have you studied everything?'

When the answer was negative, he was sent back to learn again. This back and forth between the gurukul and home went on until Swetaketu attained enlightenment.

This is what great parents do to their children. They want their children to be materially successful, but also learn the spiritual sciences and become enlightened. Do we impart such training to our kids?

For that to happen, we ourselves need to understand the value of spiritual knowledge. Only then can we pass it on to our children.

Chanakya had trained his students to be brilliant rulers of large kingdoms and empires. But he also wanted them to know that a day would come when they would have to fight the biggest war—the challenge of giving up their power and position.

It is not at all easy. If one has been in the seat of power for a long time, one gets attached to it. Yet, the greatest winner is one who can let go of that power. And if we are willingly able to let go, we have truly won the ultimate war—the war of winning over ourselves and our ego.

This is the ultimate war we need to win. The right time to learn spirituality is here and now. Let us take the first step, and the rest will follow.

We can read a spiritual book, attend a spiritual discourse (satsang), meet a spiritual master, or visit an ashram.

On a daily basis, we can measure the progress of our children's spiritual growth. Impart to them values, moral and ethics. Teach them to be strong from the inside. The foundations of life have to be spiritual.

Let this be the start of a journey within. Let all of us seek that winning mentality—the conquering of the ego and the ability to let go. Such a person can never be defeated. He is an eternal winner in every stage of life. He has won over himself—he has won the ultimate war.

Acknowledgements

I would like to acknowledge all my friends in the Indian Armed Forces who have been part of my journey in understanding the art of war. Thank you to the officers and men and women of the Indian Army, Navy, Air Force, the police service and other paramilitary forces who are working day and night to keep us safe and secure.

I am also grateful to the various defence institutions with which I have been associated: the Defence Services Staff College (DSSC), the Institute for Defence Studies and Analyses (IDSA) and the National Defence College (NDC). The same goes for the scholars and military experts continuing to research the *Arthashastra* to unearth new dimensions of war strategy.

I would like to extend a special mention to a few people who have been my friends, philosophers and guides in understanding modern-day warfare.

I would like to specially mention Wing Commander G. Aditya Kiran of the Indian Air Force and Admiral R. Gaikwad of the Indian Navy. Wing Commander G. Aditya Kiran introduced Kautilya's *Arthashastra* and my research as a subject of study at DSSC, initiating many military officers into Chanakya's art. Admiral Gaikwad too is highlighting the importance of studying the *Arthashastra* in the highest ranks of the Indian defence forces and in the public administration at NDC.

A big thank you to Colonel Pradeep Gautam (Indian Army), who has tirelessly promoted the *Arthashastra* for years. He has been organizing various conferences and seminars on the subject to create awareness at the national and international level.

I would like to thank Vice Admiral Sandeep Naithani who made me a part of the Indian Navy family—a lifelong dream of mine.

The same for D. Sivanandan, Indian Police Service (IPS) who, as the director general of Maharashtra Police and co-author of our book *Chanakya's 7 secrets of Leadership*, was instrumental in teaching me how to think strategically as is required for the elimination of crime and maintenance of law and order.

My office staff—Pranav Patel and Karthiga Thevar—and my in-house editor, Nitya Somaiya, who makes my books better before they go to my publisher's editorial team.

Acknowledgements

I would like to extend a heartfelt thank you to Penguin Random House India. Working with the editorial team led by Milee Ashwarya has been an absolute pleasure and each book has been better than the last. Thank you, Milee; you have been a friend, philosopher and guide in this journey. I thank the whole team at Penguin Random House India, including Saksham Garg and my editor Lakshmi Krishnan.

My family is my constant support. I can win any war but none against Surekha, my best half. Even before our fights start, I know she has won. My kids, Arjun (the name of the best warrior known to India from the days of the Mahabharata) and Aanvikshiki (another name by which Draupadi, a princess who herself was a war strategist, was known in the Mahabharata), deserve a special mention. Thank you to my parents C.K.K. Pillai (an author himself) and the lady who brought me to this planet, my mother, Sushila Pillai.

Finally, thank you all my readers without whom my life's mission to promote Chanakya would be incomplete.